Beyond Horizons – The Rise of the Edge AI Processing Paradigm

RIVER PUBLISHERS SERIES IN COMMUNICATIONS AND NETWORKING

The "River Publishers Series in Communications and Networking" is a series of comprehensive academic and professional books which focus on communication and network systems. Topics range from the theory and use of systems involving all terminals, computers, and information processors to wired and wireless networks and network layouts, protocols, architectures, and implementations. Also covered are developments stemming from new market demands in systems, products, and technologies such as personal communications services, multimedia systems, enterprise networks, and optical communications.

The series includes research monographs, edited volumes, handbooks and textbooks, providing professionals, researchers, educators, and advanced students in the field with an invaluable insight into the latest research and developments.

Topics included in this series include:

- Communication theory
- Multimedia systems
- Network architecture
- Optical communications
- Personal communication services
- Telecoms networks
- Wifi network protocols

For a list of other books in this series, visit www.riverpublishers.com

Beyond Horizons – The Rise of the Edge AI Processing Paradigm

Editors

Ovidiu Vermesan
SINTEF, Norway

Marcello Coppola
STMicroelectronics, France

Fabian Chersi
CEA, France

River Publishers

Routledge
Taylor & Francis Group
NEW YORK AND LONDON

Published 2025 by River Publishers
River Publishers
Broagervej 10, 9260 Gistrup, Denmark
www.riverpublishers.com

Distributed exclusively by Routledge
605 Third Avenue, New York, NY 10017, USA
4 Park Square, Milton Park, Abingdon, Oxon OX14 4RN

Beyond Horizons – The Rise of the Edge AI Processing Paradigm / by Ovidiu Vermesan, Marcello Coppola, Fabian Chersi.

ISBN: 978-87-4380-863-3 (hardback)
978-87-4380-866-4 (online)
978-87-4380-865-7 (master ebook)

DOI: 10.1201/9788743808633

Dedication

"If a machine is expected to be infallible, it cannot also be intelligent."
– Alan Turing

"Wisdom is the daughter of experience."
– Leonardo da Vinci

"Wonder is the beginning of wisdom."
– Socrates

"Education is not the learning of the facts, but the training of the mind to think."
– Albert Einstein

Acknowledgement

The editors would like to thank all the contributors for their support in the planning and preparation of this book. The recommendations and opinions expressed in the book are those of the editors, authors, and contributors and do not necessarily represent those of any organizations, employers, or companies.

Ovidiu Vermesan
Marcello Coppola
Fabian Chersi

Contents

Preface

The Dawn of Edge Intelligence Processing

This book is a journey across the landscape of edge AI technologies and applications, marking a change in how intelligent systems are designed and deployed.

The book was born from the intellectual ferment of the European Conference on EDGE AI Technologies and Applications – EEAI, held on 17-19 October 2023, Athens, Greece, offering a definitive snapshot of this transition. It provides a helpful resource for anyone seeking to comprehend the multifaceted world of edge AI, from its foundational components to its most innovative applications.

The value of the book lies in its comprehensive and in-depth exploration of the field, bridging theory with practical implementation applications.

This exploration begins by grounding the reader in a complex, high-stakes application: the advancement of autonomous vehicles for last-mile delivery. The "*Advancing Edge AI Perception Platforms and Sensor Fusion for Last-Mile Delivery Autonomous Vehicles*" chapter sets the stage by illustrating how edge AI perception platforms and sophisticated sensor fusion are essential for navigating the cluttered and unpredictable environments of the cities, thereby evolving vehicles into intelligent, software and AI-defined agents. It perfectly encapsulates the need for robust, real-time processing, a hallmark of edge computing.

Building on this practical foundation, the subsequent chapters delve into the critical enablers of edge AI technology and introduce "*AIDGE: A Framework for Deep Neural Network Development, Training and Deployment on the Edge*", a comprehensive and modular open-source framework that radically simplifies the development, training, and deployment of Deep Neural Networks across a diverse range of hardware.

This is followed by the chapter "*A Scalable and Flexible Interconnect-based Dataflow Architecture for Edge AI Inference*", a thoughtful exploration of a scalable and flexible interconnect-based dataflow architecture, a novel approach designed to accelerate the complex computations of AI inference directly on the hardware, offering significant performance gains over traditional methods.

With increased connectivity and intelligence at the edge comes the paramount concern of security. The book addresses this head-on in the chapter "*Federated Learning for Malware Detection in Edge Devices*" with a timely investigation into federated learning for malware detection. The chapter presents a solution that allows for the collaborative development of highly accurate security models without compromising user privacy or intellectual property, a critical capability for the expanding IoT ecosystem.

The collection broadens its scope to demonstrate the versatility of edge AI across different domains in the next chapter "*Image Signal Processor (ISP) Tuning using Machine Learning (ML) methods*", which details a novel ML-based method for automatically tuning ISPs, a key step for optimising camera performance in any environment.

The final chapter, "*Using Edge AI in IoT Devices for Smart Agriculture: Autonomous Weeding*", showcases the practical evolution of an autonomous weeding system for smart agriculture, highlighting the migration of complex vision algorithms to low-power, cost-effective edge devices.

Together, these six chapters provide a rich, multi-layered perspective on the state of edge AI. They describe what has been achieved and illuminate the path forward, offering the direction of a future where intelligence is seamlessly integrated into the world's fabric. The book serves as an essential guide for anyone seeking to navigate and contribute to the exciting and rapidly evolving field of edge AI.

List of Figures

List of Tables

List of Contributors

Allenet, Thibault, *CEA, France*

Bahr, Roy, *SINTEF AS, Norway*

Bichler, Olivier, *CEA, France*

Bijani, Sepehr, *NXP Semiconductors, Germany*

Brudeli, Helge, *Paxster AS, Norway*

Chersi, Fabian, *CEA, France*

Da Costa, Jean-Pierre, *University of Bordeaux, CNRS, Bordeaux Sciences Agro, France*

Deshayes, Aymeric, *University of Bordeaux, CNRS, France*

Emanuelsson, Petter, *Paxster AS, Norway*

Førrisdahl, Martin, *Paxster AS, Norway*

Germain, Christian, *University of Bordeaux, CNRS, Bordeaux Sciences Agro, France*

Keresztes, Barna, *University of Bordeaux, CNRS, Bordeaux Sciences Agro, France*

Krichene, Hana, *Université Paris-Saclay, CEA-List, France*

Kucher, Inna, *CEA, France*

Lorrain, Vincent, *CEA, France*

Moineau, Cyril, *CEA, France*

Naud, Maxence, *CEA, France*

Prasad, Rohit *Université Paris-Saclay, CEA-List, France*

Sand, Hans-Erik, *NxTECH AS, Norway*

Saxegaard, Simen Marentius, *NxTECH AS, Norway*

Serpanos, Dimitrios, *University of Patras, Greece*

Soutier, Laurent, *CEA, France*

Templier, Vincent, *CEA, France*

Vermesan, Ovidiu, *SINTEF AS, Norway*

Xenos, Georgios, *University of Patras, Greece*

1

Advancing Edge AI Perception Platforms and Sensor Fusion for Last-Mile Delivery Autonomous Vehicles

Ovidiu Vermesan[1], Roy Bahr[1], Hans-Erik Sand[2], Simen Marentius Saxegaard[2], Helge Brudeli[3], Petter Emanuelsson[3], and Martin Førrisdahl[3]

[1]SINTEF AS, Norway
[2]NxTECH AS, Norway
[3]Paxster AS, Norway

Abstract

In the rapidly evolving landscape of transportation, mobility, and logistics, the last-mile represents the final and crucial leg of the delivery journey. It involves goods travelling from a transportation hub to the ultimate destination. This is the most expensive and time-sensitive part of the supply chain business model. Challenges include navigating dense urban environments with various types of traffic participants (e.g., pedestrians, bicycles, animals, electric scooters, motorcycles, etc.), dealing with traffic congestion, locating specific delivery points, managing a high density of stops, and handling failed delivery attempts. In this context, the intersection of edge artificial intelligence (AI), autonomous systems, robotics, and sensor fusion in perception and navigation advances the development of last-mile delivery autonomous vehicle (AV) platforms that evolve towards software-defined and AI-defined vehicles (SDVs and ADVs). The advancements include multiple sensor systems for perception and communication (e.g., ultrasound, inertial, LiDAR, radar, camera, V2X, etc.), real-time data processing for localisation, and robust algorithms for navigation and interaction with diverse traffic environments. This chapter presents the concept and the implementation of an AI-based

DOI: 10.1201/9788743808633-1

perception and sensor fusion platform technical solution for autonomous last-mile delivery in controlled traffic environments.

Keywords: edge AI, perception, autonomous vehicle, sensor fusion, object recognition, last-mile delivery.

1.1 Introduction and Background

The future of mobility is intelligent, electrical, autonomous, connected, and shared, affecting all three broad types of mobility: personal mobility (moving individuals or small groups of people), mass transit (moving large numbers of people), and the movement of goods.

The last-mile of logistics refers to the final leg of the delivery journey, typically from a local distribution hub or retail centre to the end recipient's location, such as a home or business [1]. This segment is notoriously the most complex, inefficient, and expensive part of the entire supply chain, often accounting for over 50% of total delivery costs [3].

Last-mile logistics are increasingly automated, and companies that are prepared for this shift are in a stronger position to compete and take the lead. Autonomous last-mile delivery, utilising vehicles ranging from small sidewalk robots to automated vans, promises significant efficiency gains and cost reductions in logistics. As a result, various types of autonomous vehicles for last-mile delivery have emerged as follows [10] and illustrated in Figure 1.1:

- Pedestrian sidewalk vehicles. These are slow vehicles designed to travel at a pedestrian speed of 4-6 km per hour. This low speed offers improved safety and allows the operators to control the vehicle in an emergency.
- Bicycle sidewalk vehicles. These are vehicles designed to travel up to a bicycle speed of 12-15 km per hour.

Vehicle type	Pedestrian sidewalk vehicles	Bicycle sidewalk vehicles	On-road delivery vehicles
Speed (up to)	4-6 km/h	12-15 km/h	45-50 km/h
Traffic zone	Pedestrian zones	Bike paths	Road
Traffic participants	Pedestrians, cyclists, animals	Cyclists	Vehicles, cyclists

Figure 1.1 Types of vehicles for last-mile delivery.

- On-road delivery vehicles. These vehicles are built for on-road delivery at up to 45-50 km per hour. Their software algorithms and sensor systems resemble those of autonomous vehicles.

Driverless technology users utilise autonomous deliveries for several purposes:

- Delivery of goods from warehouses to stores and outlets for restocking inventory and shelves.
- Delivery of goods from stores to end consumers.
- Delivery of goods and parts between the warehouses and production facilities.

Autonomous vehicles (AVs), encompassing road-going vans and smaller sidewalk autonomous delivery vehicles, are emerging as a potentially transformative solution. By eliminating the need for a human driver, AVs offer the potential for 24/7 operation, reduced labour costs (a significant component of last-mile expense), optimised routing, and potentially lower emissions, primarily if electric. They can navigate narrow streets or pedestrian zones inaccessible to larger vehicles and improve delivery times by avoiding human-related delays.

The development of last-mile delivery autonomous vehicle fleets is linked to the evolution of Internet of Robotic Things (IoRT) platforms. IoRT serves as the technological backbone, integrating individual autonomous robotic vehicles into an interconnected system of systems. IoRT combines IoT technologies with robotics, edge computing and AI, allowing for the coordination of large-scale fleets of delivery robots that might otherwise operate alone. Connecting and integrating the last-mile delivery autonomous vehicle into fleets that are coordinated using distributed networks or IoRT platforms enables functions such as remote monitoring, intelligent communication, and the management of the entire delivery process, which can be managed from the distribution centre to the customer's doorstep. The intelligence and real-time responsiveness of the autonomous delivery fleets and the IoRT platforms are significantly enhanced by edge AI. Edge AI embeds data processing and decision-making capabilities directly onto the vehicles themselves, strengthening the processing capabilities and the analytics of each vehicle in the fleet or the IoRT platform. The use of edge AI enables continuous route optimisation, obstacles and traffic participants avoidance, and real-time adaptation to changing environmental conditions, which are critical for navigating pedestrian spaces and complex urban environments safely and efficiently. Edge AI-powered robotics within the IoRT framework

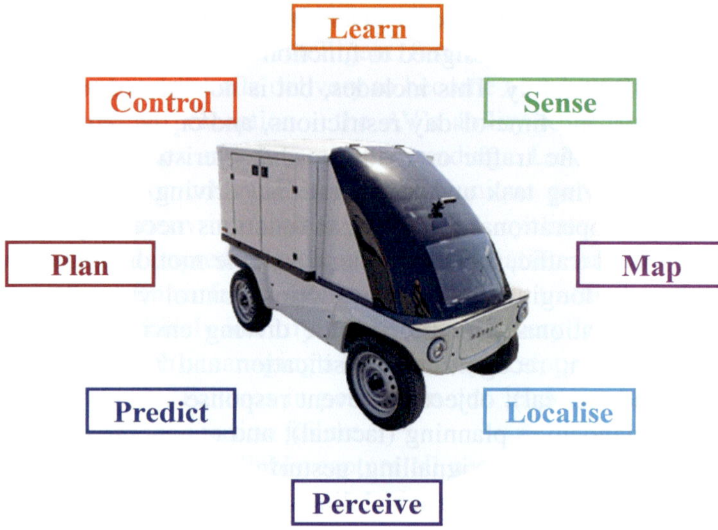

Figure 1.2 Autonomous vehicle functional elements.

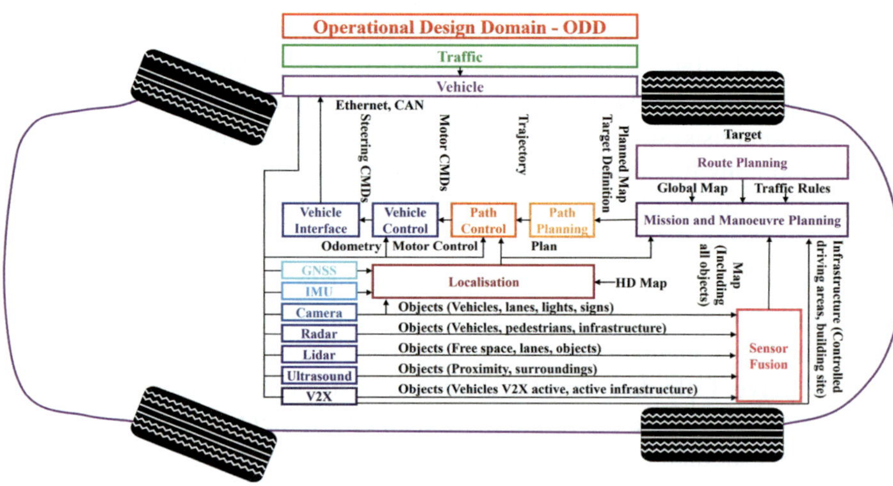

Figure 1.3 Autonomous vehicle functional architecture overview. Source: Adapted from [7].

The scalable functional architecture implements different autonomous functions using AI-based platforms that can navigate autonomously, detecting dynamic obstacles and following an optimal trajectory. The vehicles can recognise actions by processing information acquired from perception sensors and sensor fusion (e.g., GNSS, IMU, camera, radar, LiDAR, V2X). The processes are integrated into the ROS architecture, which shows potential for last-mile delivery autonomous vehicles applications.

The development of last-mile autonomous delivery vehicles is following the latest advances in SDVs to manage and integrate multiple software stacks and hardware components from various suppliers. The convergence of SDV, generative AI, and the Internet of Things (IoT) can pave the way for AI-defined vehicles as the future of mobility [32]. ADVs are the next step in the development of SDVs, focusing on hardware and infrastructure advancements that enable software decoupling from hardware with a hybrid stack that integrates control, processing and AI functionalities seamlessly [32, 34].

1.2 Sensor Fusion in Last-Mile Context

Sensor fusion is the process of intelligently combining data from multiple heterogeneous sensors [14] to generate a more accurate, complete, reliable, and robust representation of the environment than any single sensor operating alone. It leverages the complementary strengths of different sensor modalities while mitigating their weaknesses.

In the specific context of last-mile delivery, sensor fusion aims to build a detailed and dynamic understanding of the immediate surroundings, which is crucial for navigating complex, often cluttered, and highly interactive environments, such as sidewalks, crosswalks, residential streets, and building entrances [15]. Key objectives include:

- Accurate localisation and mapping, especially in GNSS-challenged urban canyons [16].
- Robust detection and tracking of static and dynamic obstacles, including pedestrians, cyclists, pets, and other small, unpredictable actors common in urban/suburban settings [18].
- Reliable perception across diverse and challenging conditions, such as varying lighting (day/night, shadows, glare, etc.), adverse weather (rain, fog, snow, etc.), and sensor occlusions [21].
- Precise identification of navigable paths, drivable surfaces, curbs, and specific delivery locations (e.g., doorsteps, designated drop-off zones) [18].
- Generating a unified environmental model suitable for real-time planning and control of potentially low-speed, highly manoeuvrable delivery vehicles [22].

A typical sensor suite for a last-mile delivery autonomous vehicle aims to provide 360-degree awareness and redundancy by combining sensors with different operating principles and characteristics.

Common sensors components for last-mile delivery autonomous vehicles are presented in the Table 1.1 and described in the following paragraphs.

Cameras are the primary source of rich semantic information for autonomous vehicles [18]. They capture visual details like colour, texture, and shape, enabling the recognition and classification of objects (pedestrians, vehicles, traffic signs, traffic lights, lane markings), interpretation of road signs, and potentially reading delivery labels or house numbers [3]. Cameras provide high-resolution data, are relatively low-cost compared to LiDAR, are passive sensors consuming less power, and are adept at capturing the complex visual details necessary for semantic understanding in diverse urban and pedestrian environments [18]. Their cost-effectiveness is a significant advantage for deploying delivery robots or vans at scale. Multiple cameras can provide a 360-degree field of view [18]. Camera performance degrades significantly in adverse weather conditions (e.g., heavy rain, fog, snow) and challenging lighting (e.g., low light, nighttime, direct glare, shadows) [18]. Monocular cameras struggle with direct and accurate depth estimation, requiring computationally intensive techniques like stereo vision or structure-from-motion or fusion with other sensors like LiDAR or radar. They are susceptible to occlusions, where objects of interest are hidden behind others. Fast motion or vehicle vibration can cause motion blur, particularly with rolling-shutter cameras, potentially impacting the accuracy of perception [18]. Cameras are indispensable for navigating visually complex sidewalks and streets, identifying pedestrians and other vulnerable road users (VRUs) for safe interaction, reading traffic signals and signs crucial for road crossings, and potentially identifying specific delivery addresses or drop-off points [18]. However, the limitations in poor weather and lighting pose significant challenges for achieving reliable 24/7 operation required by many delivery services. While global shutter cameras can mitigate motion blur in dynamic close-quarters environments, they also add to the cost [18]. The need for robust performance across diverse environmental conditions necessitates fusing camera data with other sensor modalities.

LiDAR is the primary sensor for generating accurate, high-resolution 3D maps of the environment and providing precise distance measurements of objects [3]. It creates a point cloud representing the geometry of the surroundings. LiDAR offers excellent depth accuracy and creates detailed 3D

Table 1.1 Sensor Modality Comparison for Last-Mile Delivery AVs

Feature	Camera	LiDAR	Radar	IMU	Ultrasound	V2X
Role	Semantic understanding, object classification, traffic sign, light recognition.	Accurate 3D mapping, depth perception, obstacle geometry.	Detect objects and measure their distance, velocity, and angle in relation to the vehicle.	Motion/ orientation tracking, dead reckoning during GNSS loss.	Very short-range object detection, parking, docking assist.	Extended situational awareness, cooperative perception, non-line-of-sight detection.
Strengths (Last-Mile)	Rich detail for VRU and sign recognition, low cost, low power.	Precise localisation in urban canyons, detects low obstacles, curbs, day, night operation.	Robust performance at distance. Not significantly affected by rain, fog, snow, low-light, night conditions.	Operates without external signals (GPS-denied), high frequency data for fusion/ stabilization.	Very low cost, detects objects extremely close (blind spots), good for tight manoeuvring.	Detects beyond line-of-sight, integrated with infrastructure (e.g. traffic lights).
Limitations (Last-Mile)	Poor performance in bad weather, lighting, poor depth estimation, motion blur.	High cost (major barrier), degraded by heavy precipitation, dust, no colour, texture info.	Lower resolution image of the environment, poor to detect and classify stationary objects, inference from other radars.	Accumulates drift error quickly, needs constant correction, sensitive to vibration/temp.	Very limited range (<5-10m), poor angular resolution, poor performance at speed.	Requires widespread adoption, infrastructure, latency, reliability issues, security, privacy concerns.

Table 1.1 *Continued.*

Feature	Camera	LiDAR	Radar	IMU	Ultrasound	V2X
Cost Factor	Low	High and decreasing.	Medium and lower than that of LiDAR systems.	Low (MEMS) to medium.	Very low.	Medium (requires comms module + potential network, infrastructure costs).
Importance for Last-Mile	Essential (semantics, VRUs, signs).	Highly important (localisation, 3D structure, obstacle detection)	Still expensive. Reliable object detection / tracking in poor weather / lighting conditions.	Essential (localisation continuity, state estimation)	Complementary (near-field safety, docking)	Potentially high (safety, efficiency), but dependent on ecosystem maturity.

representations, which are crucial for localisation, mapping, and obstacle detection [21]. It operates effectively regardless of ambient lighting conditions (day or night) [21]. Its performance is generally more robust in certain adverse weather conditions (like light rain or fog) compared to cameras, although heavy precipitation can still cause significant degradation [21]. Recent advancements have led to more compact and potentially lower-cost solid-state LiDAR units. LiDAR sensors remain relatively expensive, particularly high-resolution, long-range units, posing a significant cost barrier for mass deployment, especially on more miniature, cost-sensitive delivery robots [4]. Performance can be degraded by heavy rain, snow, dust, or fog [21]. LiDAR cannot perceive colour or texture information, making it challenging to classify objects based solely on LiDAR data (e.g., reading traffic signs or distinguishing between visually similar objects) [23]. The point clouds generated can be sparse, especially for distant or small objects. Mutual interference between multiple LiDAR sensors operating in the same area is a potential issue. Traditional mechanical scanning LiDARs have moving parts, raising concerns about long-term reliability and durability, particularly on vehicles operating over bumpy terrain, such as sidewalks. LiDAR is crucial for precise localisation and mapping within complex urban canyons or sidewalk environments where GPS may be unreliable [21]. It excels at detecting low-lying obstacles, curbs, potholes, or changes in terrain that might be missed by cameras alone. The high cost remains a significant challenge for the last-mile business case [4]. The typically lower speeds and shorter operational ranges in last-mile delivery may allow for the use of lower-cost, shorter-range LiDAR sensors compared to those needed for high-speed highway autonomy [14]. Fusion with cameras is essential to add semantic understanding to LiDAR's geometric data.

Radar sensors [19] are one of the key elements for the autonomous vehicle's perception system due to their resilience to adverse environmental conditions. Radar can see through darkness and fog, and to a certain extent through rain, and snow, conditions that severely challenge or blind other sensors, such as cameras. This capability ensures a baseline of operational safety and functionality, regardless of the time of day or weather conditions, providing data on the range, velocity, and angle of other objects with a high degree of accuracy. The synergistic integration of high-frequency radar, 5G communication, and multimodal radar technologies greatly enhances the sensing capability and environmental adaptability of autonomous vehicle perception systems [20]. However, radars present a few challenges. In heavy rainfalls, the radio signals can suffer from attenuation, slightly reducing their effective range. Additionally, in dense urban environments, the radio waves can bounce off multiple surfaces before returning to the sensor. This multi-path reflection, or clutter, can create "ghost" targets, misleading the vehicle's perception system into “thinking” an object is present where there is none. The resolution of radar makes it challenging to classify objects with certainty, as it for examples struggles to distinguish between a pedestrian, a cyclist, or a stationary object, such as a signpost, based on its signature alone.

These challenges are particularly amplified in the context of last-mile delivery for autonomous vehicles. The ODD for these vehicles involves navigating complex and cluttered environments such as residential streets, sidewalks, and loading zones. Standard automotive radars are optimised for detecting large metallic objects, such as other vehicles, and may fail to reliably detect smaller, low-profile, or non-metallic items in these areas, including delivery packages, curbs, children's toys, or pets. The proximity to buildings, parked vehicles, and other street furniture exacerbates the multi-path reflection problem, making it more challenging to maintain a clear and accurate perception of the immediate surroundings.

IMUs measure the vehicle's linear acceleration and angular velocity using accelerometers and gyroscopes [16]. This data is integrated over time to estimate changes in velocity, position, and orientation (roll, pitch, yaw). They are fundamental for state estimation and enable dead reckoning navigation during periods when external positioning signals, such as GPS, are unavailable [16]. IMUs provide high-frequency motion data (often 100 Hz or higher), completely independent of external signals or environmental conditions, allowing continuous operation in tunnels, urban canyons, dense foliage, or indoors [16]. They are relatively low-cost, especially Micro-Electro-Mechanical Systems (MEMS) based units, compact, and consume little power [16]. IMU data is critical for stabilising perception data from other sensors (compensating for vehicle motion) and for providing the motion inputs needed for sensor fusion algorithms, such as Kalman filters [24]. The primary limitation of IMUs is drift, minor errors in acceleration and angular velocity measurements accumulate over time, leading to rapidly increasing errors in the estimated position and orientation [16]. This necessitates frequent corrections using absolute positioning sensors (such as GPS) or relative positioning derived from other sensors (e.g., LiDAR/camera-based SLAM). IMUs are sensitive to temperature changes and vibrations, which can affect their accuracy [16]. Accurate calibration is crucial, but it can be complex [16]. Magnetometers, sometimes included for heading reference, are unreliable in urban environments due to magnetic interference from buildings, vehicles, and infrastructure [25]. IMUs are indispensable for last-mile navigation due to frequent GPS signal degradation or loss in urban canyons, underpasses, or near tall buildings [16]. The high-frequency data helps maintain a smooth estimate of the vehicle's state, which is crucial for controlling robots navigating potentially uneven sidewalks or making frequent stops and starts. Cost-effective MEMS IMUs are generally sufficient, but robust fusion with GPS, LiDAR-SLAM, or visual odometry is essential to bind the inherent drift [16].

Ultrasonic sensors use high-frequency sound waves to detect the presence and distance of objects at very short ranges [26]. They operate on the principle of measuring the time-of-flight of emitted sound pulses reflecting off nearby objects. They are relatively inexpensive and easy to integrate. They can detect objects close to the vehicle (within a few meters), effectively covering blind spots often missed by cameras or LiDAR [23]. Their performance is largely unaffected by lighting conditions (work in darkness) or the colour/transparency of the object [27]. They are relatively robust in some adverse weather conditions [27]. Ultrasound sensors have a minimal detection range, of up to 4-5 meters depending on the sensor and conditions [26]. Their angular resolution is poor due to broad beam patterns, making it difficult to distinguish between closely spaced objects, determine object shape, or precisely locate small objects [27]. Performance degrades significantly at higher vehicle speeds [23]. They can be susceptible to interference from external ultrasonic noise sources [28]. They may struggle to detect soft, sound-absorbing materials [27]. Their primary utility in last-mile delivery is for low-speed, close-quarters manoeuvring, such as parking assistance for vans, docking at a specific delivery point, navigating very narrow passages, or detecting immediate low-lying obstacles like curbs right next to the vehicle or robot [26]. They can serve as a safety sensor for detecting the presence of people near loading doors [29]. Due to their limited range and resolution, they are unsuitable for primary navigation or obstacle avoidance at typical operational speeds but serve as a valuable, cost-effective complementary sensor for near-field safety and precision manoeuvring.

V2X encompasses technologies (primarily DSRC/IEEE 802.11p and C-V2X/cellular) that enable vehicles to communicate wirelessly with other vehicles (V2V), roadside infrastructure (V2I), pedestrians (V2P, often via smartphones), and the network or cloud (V2N) [30]. Its key role in perception is enabling cooperative perception, where sensor data and derived information are shared among connected entities [30]. V2X can dramatically extend a vehicle's perception range and awareness beyond the line-of-sight limitations of its onboard sensors [30]. By sharing data (raw sensor data, processed object lists, or intent information), vehicles can "see" around corners or through obstructions via the sensors of other connected agents. V2I communication can provide critical information, such as traffic signal phase and timing (SPaT), road hazard warnings, and work zone alerts [30]. This enhanced situational awareness can significantly improve safety and traffic efficiency, enabling coordinated manoeuvres such as platooning [30]. C-V2X offers the potential advantage of leveraging existing cellular infrastructure for V2N, potentially providing more exhaustive coverage compared to DSRC's reliance on dedicated Roadside Units (RSUs) [31]. The effectiveness of V2X, particularly V2V and V2I for cooperative perception, heavily depends on widespread adoption and deployment – a significant network effect challenge. Communication channels have limitations in terms of latency, reliability, bandwidth, and range, which can affect the timeliness and quality of shared perception data. Ensuring the security and authenticity of V2X messages is paramount to prevent malicious attacks (e.g., false hazard warnings, Sybil attacks) [30]. Privacy concerns exist regarding the sharing of vehicle data. Standardisation is still evolving, with ongoing debate and regional differences between DSRC (IEEE 802.11p/ITS-G5) and C-V2X (LTE-V2X, 5G-V2X) hindering global interoperability [31]. Deploying the necessary infrastructure (RSUs for DSRC, potentially upgraded cellular networks for C-V2X) involves significant cost and effort. Cooperative perception via V2X is potentially very valuable in dense, occluded urban environments typical of last-mile routes, allowing a delivery robot or van to perceive pedestrians or vehicles hidden from its direct view [30]. V2I communication providing traffic light status is crucial for safe intersection negotiation. V2N connectivity can be used for real-time updates to delivery routes, receiving customer instructions, remote monitoring, or potentially teleoperation under challenging situations. However, reliable connectivity (cellular or RSU coverage) might be inconsistent across all delivery zones, including dense urban areas or more remote suburban neighbourhoods. Security is especially critical for autonomous delivery vehicles, as it prevents theft, hijacking, or disruption of service.

GNSS plays a key role in autonomous last-mile delivery vehicles by providing essential positioning, navigation, and timing information. It enables these vehicles to accurately determine their location and navigate to delivery destinations, facilitating efficient route optimisation and real-time tracking. One of the primary strengths of GNSS is its global coverage, enabling positioning data to be available virtually anywhere. Its high accuracy, especially when complemented by augmentation systems like Real-Time Kinematic (RTK), can achieve centimetre-level precision, which is essential for operating in complex urban environments. Additionally, GNSS provides real-time data updates that support continuous adjustments during deliveries, making it a cost-effective solution widely available for implementation. GNSS has limitations as signal interference can occur in urban environments, where buildings or tunnels obstruct satellite signals, leading to degraded performance. Multipath effects, where signals bounce off surfaces, can further compromise accuracy. Latency issues may arise, affecting the system's responsiveness in dynamic traffic situations, and extreme weather conditions or satellite outages may challenge the reliability of GNSS. To effectively utilise GNSS in last-mile delivery vehicles, specific requirements must be met. Integrating GNSS with other technologies, such as inertial navigation systems (INS), LiDAR, and cameras, is vital for enhancing accuracy and reliability. Robust software algorithms are needed to process GNSS data and compensate for environmental errors. Energy-efficient solutions are essential to ensure continuous operation without overburdening the vehicle's power resources.

Real-time data exchange must be established to optimise routes and ensure safety while also adhering to safety standards compliance.

1.3 Autonomous Vehicle Architecture for Last-Mile Delivery

Autonomous vehicle for transport of goods considers the use of scalable processing capabilities at the edge with AI-based functions implemented into the perception domain and covering the edge computing capabilities implemented into vehicles of different sizes using the same generic architecture as illustrated in Figure 1.4 [7].

1.3.1 Localisation and High-Definition Map

Localisation is critical for the safe and efficient operation of last-mile delivery autonomous vehicles. By employing high-definition (HD) maps that detail urban infrastructure, such as road types, curb locations, and traffic signals, these vehicles can navigate complex environments more effectively.

The maps incorporate real-time data updates to reflect changing road conditions, enhancing navigational accuracy and safety.

1.3.2 Perception Implementation

Perception in last-mile delivery autonomous vehicles integrates AI to identify and classify various objects within the vehicle's vicinity. This involves

Figure 1.4 Vehicles and scalability. Source: [7].

Cloud library, and YOLO, and AI-based computing platforms like NVIDIA Jetson AGX Orin, were evaluated for integration into different layers of autonomous vehicle architecture.

These AI-based frameworks, algorithms, libraries, and platforms were utilised during various phases of the autonomous vehicle platform demonstrator's development.

The decision-making relies on sensor fusion and AI processing.

Furthermore, the vehicle platform features several actuators and control units, including the electric steering servo and throttle/speed control for autonomous driving, speech information/recognition for use-case service/security purposes, NFC/mobile locking/unlocking systems, and wireless/wired emergency stops for safety reasons.

Perception sensors and navigation

The platform was integrated with the NVIDIA Jetson AGC Orin, which provides AI-based perception and sensor fusion capabilities [9]. To abstract the sensor brand and interface from Orin, parsing of the ultrasonic sensor electronic control unit (ECU) data were implemented and an interface provided (independent of ultrasonic system used).

Having the vehicle control unit (VCU) interpret the sensor data also enables it to have an emergency brake function. This function is set so that if the vehicle is autonomous mode, the vehicle's VCU sends a signal to disable drive to the CAN relay, which in turn triggers engaging of the electronic park brake.

To get the ultrasonic sensors to have an impact on the vehicle motion there needs to be several interfaces defined where the data and information can flow. There are two distinct types of interfaces in form of CAN and ROS topics. An illustration of the interfaces is given in Figure 1.8.

The ultrasonic sensor hardware abstraction layer (HAL) provides an interface that includes the CAN output from the VCU interface but provides it as an ROS topic that other nodes inside NVIDIA Jetson AGX Orin platform can make use of. The topic is described in a message and provides information for each sensor in a separate variable.

Tracking System for Platooning

Platooning of autonomous vehicles refers to a formation of multiple autonomous vehicles travelling closely together in a single-file line, with the lead vehicle controlling the speed and direction for the following vehicles. The group of connected autonomous vehicles exchange information, allowing

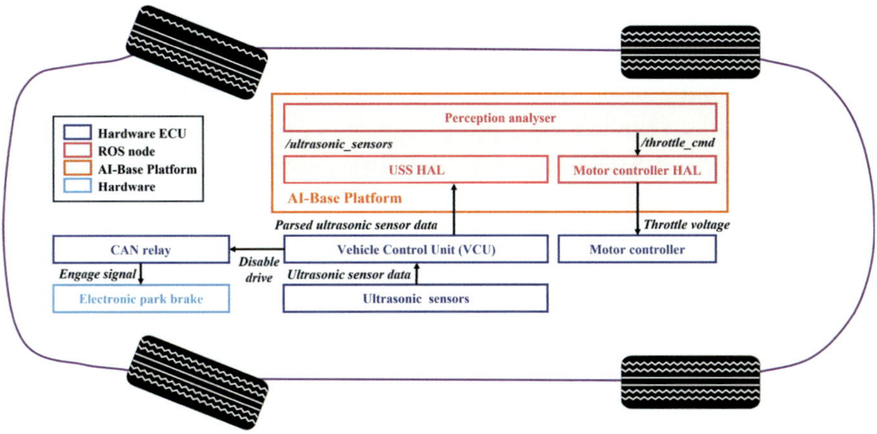

Figure 1.8 System overview. Source: Adapted from [9].

them to drive in a coordinated manner, with very small spacings, while still travelling safely at relatively high speeds [36].

The fleets of last-mile delivery autonomous vehicles utilise platooning coordinated driving style to enhance logistics efficiency, increase road capacity, improve traffic flow, reduce delivery times, and load goods from common warehouse hubs.

Platooning requires the development of robust and reliable V2V communication, multi-sensor perception systems, control algorithms, and infrastructure, including dedicated lanes or specific road configurations, to function optimally.

Information on the vehicles' speeds, positions, accelerations, decelerations, and other relevant data for the vehicles in the platoon, as well as for those joining or leaving the platoon, is crucial, as all the vehicles in the platoon need to react efficiently and safely in real-time.

Several information flow topologies (IFTs) have been traditionally used in the literature, such as predecessor-following (PF), two-predecessor-following (TPF), and bidirectional (BDL). The advancement of communication systems increased the use of more general schemes such as r-predecessor following (rPLF). The dynamic platoon nature, with vehicles changing their relative position over time, also adds complexity to the topology of communications [36].

The platooning style of driving can be implemented for autonomous vehicles equipped with V2X connectivity by conveying traffic information (e.g.,

GNSS, speed, or signal timing) and using either unlicensed V2X (ITS-G5) or cellular V2X (LTE-V2X/NR-V2X) [37].

The platooning of last-mile delivery autonomous vehicles can be implemented using the vehicle's perception sensors (e.g., cameras, ultrasound) for areas with good visibility, and an alternative solution can complement the V2X system.

The following section presents the implementation of a tracking system for platooning, as demonstrated in the ECSEL JU AI4CSM project [9], utilising an NVIDIA Jetson AGX Orin processing platform running the Ubuntu Linux operating system, which offers AI capabilities for the vehicle's perception domain. The vehicle's onboard unit communicates with its sensors through the ROS operating system as middleware.

The autonomous vehicle, illustrated in the Figure 1.15, is equipped with multiple perception sensors, including LiDAR, a depth camera, and ultrasound sensors.

For the implementation, the Intel RealSense D455 RGB-D depth camera was used as a sensor to detect the logo mark placed on the rear of the lead vehicle, serving as a target for the follower vehicle to follow.

The logo in Figure 1.9 is attached to the rear of the vehicle. The logo design can make it difficult to distinguish it from other circular objects or signs with straight lines within the circle, such as no stopping/parking signs.

To detect the logo, two different detection model frameworks were tested, YOLOv5 [38] and YOLOv8 [39]. YOLO is a computer vision model developed by Ultralytics and is part of the "You Only Look Once" (YOLO) family of models, known for their high inference speed, making them suitable for

Figure 1.9 Tracking system logo and no stopping/parking sign.

real-time applications. Both frameworks are implemented in PyTorch, which contributes to their ease of use, speed, and accuracy.

YOLOv8 is a further development of YOLOv5, not only in terms of detection architecture but also in the development framework. YOLOv8 provides enhanced documentation and a streamlined setup for training and deploying a detection model. The use case presented in this paper addresses the training of a simple detection model. As a result, the nano model for both YOLOv5 and YOLOv8 was used, as it provides optimal inference speed and an architecture suitable for our detection problem.

To create an effective detection model, the dataset is the most critical factor. Datasets with diverse photos, logos on vehicles, and t-shirts in different lighting conditions were collected for training the models.

The base dataset contains approximately 1000 images, where 10% of the pictures do not contain any logos, as many false positives were encountered during training on images with logos only.

Augmentation techniques are critical when training a robust model. YOLOv5 and YOLOv8 models have built-in augmentation techniques, which we utilised with the default settings. In addition to the built-in augmentation techniques, we augmented the dataset by pasting logos onto images from images recorded with a vehicle, as illustrated in Figure 1.10.

The training results for the best-performing YOLOv5 and YOLOv8 models showed that training for YOLOv8 is more stable. The mAP (mean Average Precision) metric for object detection, mAP50-0.95, converges to a higher value for YOLOv8, indicating that the model can predict the correct class with greater confidence.

To enhance the system's robustness, a tracking algorithm was implemented on top of the detection model. The tracking algorithm is built into YOLOv8, which is the ByteTrack AI algorithm [39].

The algorithm can detect and continuously track multiple objects by assigning each one a unique ID, considering all detected objects (not just high-confidence ones), which can improve its tracking accuracy even in challenging conditions, such as occlusion.

The ByteTrack AI algorithm can be applied directly, with no final tuning required, using only the bounding boxes with pixel-level information from the detection model. Figure 1.11 illustrates a constructed case where two logos appear. Since tracking is implemented, the following vehicle knows which one to follow, as it has an assigned leader ID.

This implementation makes the system more robust against false positives, as these will receive unique IDs, and the following vehicle is locked to its leader's ID.

Figure 1.10 Logos pasted on driving data.

Figure 1.11 The detection and tracking module returning one unique bounding box.

1.3.3 Prediction, Decision-Making, Planning and Route Optimisation

The last-mile delivery autonomous vehicles decision-making framework utilises predictive algorithms to assess potential interactions and outcomes based on current vehicle positioning and environmental factors. By analysing previously collected data, these vehicles can efficiently plan paths that minimize risks and enhance delivery speed. Planning algorithms incorporate multi-layered decision-making processes that prioritize safety and operational efficiency.

Through machine learning algorithms, AI assesses historical data, including traffic patterns and weather conditions, to optimize delivery routes. This reduces delivery times and operational costs, allowing for quicker and more efficient deliveries.

1.3.3.1 Odometry and path planning

Vehicles with rear-wheel drive and front-wheel steering, is referred to as Ackermann steering. When the vehicle makes a turn, the wheel on the outer side of the turn has a slightly larger turning radius than the wheel on the inner side. The sharper the turn, the greater the difference in turning radii between the wheels.

Most vehicles, uses kingpins to control each wheel, with a single servo to control the vehicle's heading. In an Ackermann-steered vehicle, the heading can be simplified to a bicycle model, where the average angle of the front wheels is directly correlated with the vehicle's heading. The inner and outer wheel angle is different depending on left or right turn (counterclockwise or clockwise turns) and must be taken into considerations during the odometry and path planning development. Odometry, based on sensor fusion and the data from the integrated motion sensors, is used to estimate the position over time and improve the position accuracy, velocity and attitude.

The configuration is illustrated in Figure 1.12, where $\emptyset$ is the steering angle of the front wheels. For our scenario the steering angle of the front wheels $\emptyset$ is derived from the pure pursuit equation and given below [50, 51], where $\overrightarrow{y}$ is the vector pointing from the rear axle to the camera, $\overrightarrow{z}$ is the vector pointing from rear axle to the tracked object (tuneable look-ahead), and $\overrightarrow{L}_a$ is the length of wheelbase.

$$\emptyset = \frac{2L_a}{|\overrightarrow{z}|}\sqrt{1 - \left(\frac{\overrightarrow{y}\,\overrightarrow{z}}{|\overrightarrow{y}||\overrightarrow{z}|}\right)^2} \tag{1.1}$$

and intervene when necessary. This hybrid approach helps manage the unexpected challenges presented by complex urban environments.

Safety strategies for last-mile delivery autonomous vehicles involve redundant systems to prevent malfunction and protocols for engaging human overseers in critical situations. Security considerations also encompass the protection of data communication between vehicles and management systems to prevent unauthorized access and ensure operational integrity.

1.4 Edge AI Platforms

In the context of autonomous vehicles, an edge AI platform refers to the integrated hardware, software, and edge AI stack, as well as the data responsible for executing the complex computational tasks required to perform autonomous functions and intelligent decision-making. This includes processing vast amounts of sensor data, running sophisticated AI algorithms for perception, sensor fusion, localisation, path planning, and motion control, and ultimately making real-time driving decisions.

For last-mile delivery AVs, the definition of an AI platform is heavily influenced by the specific constraints of the application. Delivery vehicles, robots and smaller vans operate under stringent size, weight, power, and cost constraints compared to larger robotaxis or trucks.

This requires highly optimised, edge-computing platforms. High-performance Graphics Processing Units (GPUs) are used for training and complex inference, while autonomous vehicle platforms rely on GPUs and specialised, power-efficient AI accelerators such as Field-Programmable Gate Arrays (FPGAs), Neural Processing Units (NPUs), Tensor Processing Units (TPUs), or custom ASICs integrated into System-on-a-Chip (SoC). NVIDIA's Jetson AGX Orin platform is an example targeted at such edge applications, including last-mile delivery vehicles and robots.

The software stack typically runs on a real-time operating system (RTOS) or a standard OS like Linux with real-time extensions, often utilising middleware like ROS for modularity and communication between different software components (perception, planning, control).

The platform hosts the AI libraries (e.g., TensorFlow, PyTorch, etc.) and the specific algorithms implementing the vehicle's autonomous capabilities. The key distinction for last-mile AI platforms is the focus on energy efficiency, computational density, and cost-effectiveness, which are suitable for scalable deployment on smaller, battery-powered vehicles.

1.4.1 Robot Operating System

ROS is not a traditional operating system in the sense of Windows or Linux. Instead, it is a flexible framework of software libraries and tools that simplify the creation of complex robot applications [45, 46].

ROS is an open-source framework for writing robot software, providing a collection of tools, libraries, and conventions that aim to simplify the task of creating complex and robust robot behaviour across a wide variety of robotic platforms. It has also been recently used in autonomous vehicles, as seen in the case of this implementation for last-mile delivery autonomous vehicles and other autonomous systems. ROS is rather a middleware, a set of software frameworks for robot software development [35, 40, 47, 48].

There are two versions of ROS: ROS 1, which evolved with community contributions, and ROS 2, released in 2017. ROS 2 incorporates real-time capabilities, improved security, and better support for distributed systems by leveraging the Data Distribution Service (DDS) standard [15]. A table of key differences between ROS 1 and ROS 2 can be seen in Table 1.2 [11].

ROS provides services expected from an operating system, including hardware abstraction, low-level device control, implementation of commonly

Table 1.2 Summary of ROS 2 Features Compared to ROS 1 [11]

Category	ROS 1	ROS 2
Network Transport	Tailored protocol built on TCP/UDP	Existing standard (DDS), with abstraction supporting addition of others
Network Architecture	Central name server (roscore)	Peer-to-peer discovery
Platform Support	Linux	Linux, Windows, macOS
Client Libraries	Written independently in each language	Sharing a common underlying C library (rcl)
Node vs. Process	Single node per process	Multiple nodes per process
Threading Model	Callback queues and handlers	Swappable executor
Node State Management	None	Lifecycle nodes
Embedded Systems	The ROSSerial client library used for small, embedded devices	The micro-ROS stack integrates microcontrollers with standard ROS 2
Parameter Access	Auxiliary protocol built on XMLRPC	Implemented using service calls
Parameter Types	Type inferred when assigned	Type declared and enforced

used functionality, message passing between processes, and package management.

The core of ROS is its anonymous publish/ subscribe messaging system. A process (called a "node") that has information to share can publish it to a specific "topic". Other nodes interested in that type of information can subscribe to the topic to receive the messages, which creates a modular, decoupled architecture where different parts of the system can be developed and tested independently [42, 43] .

The integration of ROS into autonomous vehicles involves several key aspects, such as [41]:

- **Hardware abstraction**, where ROS provides a standardised interface to a wide variety of sensors and actuators, meaning that a high-level autonomous driving algorithm can be developed independently of the specific hardware being used. In this context, a "LiDAR driver" node could publish data from a particular brand of LiDAR to a standardised topic, and a perception node could subscribe to that topic without needing to know the specifics of the LiDAR hardware.
- **Inter-process communication**: Autonomous vehicles have a multitude of processes running concurrently: perception, localisation, planning, and control. ROS's messaging system allows these processes to communicate with each other in a reliable and time-synchronised manner, even if they are running on different computers within the vehicle.
- **Ecosystem and tools**: ROS has an ecosystem of tools for visualisation, simulation, and data logging. Tools like RViz enable developers to visualise sensor data and the vehicle's state in 3D, while Gazebo provides a realistic simulation environment for testing algorithms without requiring a physical vehicle.

ROS is used as a platform for developing perception and sensor fusion systems [49] in the implementation of the last-mile delivery autonomous vehicle presented in this chapter.

As a result, several features of the platform were analysed, evaluated and integrated into the vehicle architecture. These elements are described below:

- **AI integration**: The modular nature of ROS makes it easy to integrate AI and machine learning libraries. The typical approach used was to have a ROS node that utilises a library such as TensorFlow or PyTorch to perform object detection or semantic segmentation on camera images. The results of this process (e.g., the locations of other vehicles and pedestrians) were then published to a ROS topic for other nodes to use.

- **Sensor fusion**: The implemented autonomous vehicles rely on a variety of sensors, including cameras, LiDAR, ultrasound, IMUs, etc. ROS provided a framework for fusing the data from these different sensors to create a more accurate and robust understanding of the environment. A "sensor fusion" node could subscribe to topics containing data from the camera, LiDAR, and IMU, and then use a filter (like a Kalman filter) to combine this data and produce a unified representation of the environment.

The original implementation of the functions for the last-mile delivery autonomous vehicles was implemented in the original version of ROS (ROS 1). The test results show that the system has some limitations in terms of real-time performance and security, and the newer version, ROS 2 [44, 45], is integrated into the new vehicle design due to the following [35]:

- **Real-time capabilities**: ROS 2 is built on top of the DDS standard, which provides real-time, reliable, and scalable communication. The capabilities are necessary for autonomous vehicle implementation to reduce delays and increase the system's robustness.
- **Security**: ROS 2 includes a better security framework that provides features like authentication, encryption, and access control, which are essential for protecting the vehicle from cyberattacks.
- **Quality of Service (QoS)**: ROS 2 allows specifying QoS policies for each publisher and subscriber, which enables the control of aspects like reliability, durability, and latency, ensuring that critical data is delivered in a timely and reliable manner.

A set of principles and specific requirements guides the design of ROS 2, including distribution, abstraction, asynchrony, and modularity, as well as several design requirements such as security, integration of embedded systems, use of diverse communication networks, real-time computing, and product readiness.

The ROS 2 APIs provide access to communication patterns, such as services and actions, which are organised under the concept of a node. ROS 2 also provides APIs for parameters, timers, launch, and other auxiliary tools, which can be used to design a robotic system. ROS 2 issues a request-response style pattern, known as services. Request-response communication provides a clear association between a request and its corresponding response, which can be helpful when ensuring that a task was completed or received. A unique communication pattern of ROS 2 is the action. Actions are goal-oriented and asynchronous, providing communication interfaces with request-response capabilities, periodic feedback, and the ability to be cancelled. The middleware architecture of ROS 2 consists of several abstraction layers distributed across many decoupled packages. These abstraction layers enable multiple solutions for the required functionality, such as various middleware or logging solutions. Additionally, the distribution across various packages allows users to replace components or take only the necessary pieces of the system, which may be important for certification [11, 12].

Figure 1.14 displays the layers within ROS 2 as it is a set of software libraries and tools for building robot and autonomous systems applications. ROS2 builds upon DDS and contains a DDS abstraction layer. Users do not need to be aware of the DDS APIs due to this abstraction layer. This layer enables ROS2 to have high-level configurations and optimises the utilisation of DDS. Additionally, due to the use of DDS, ROS2 does not require a master process [7, 11, 12].

The client libraries provide access to the core communication APIs. They are tailored to each programming language to make them more idiomatic and take advantage of language-specific features. Communication is agnostic to how the system is distributed across compute resources, whether they are in the same process, a different process, or even a different processing unit. A

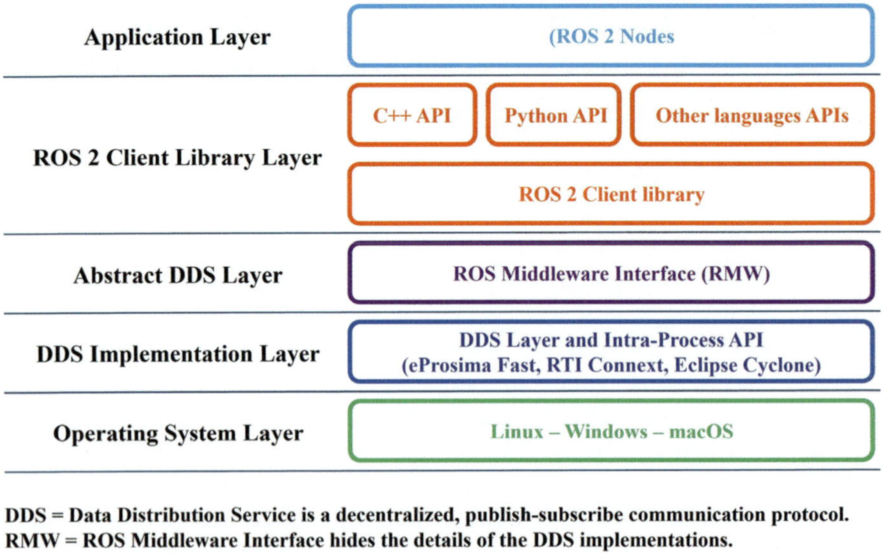

Figure 1.14 ROS 2 architecture [7, 12].

user may distribute their application across multiple machines and processes, and even leverage cloud compute resources, with minimal changes to the source code. ROS 2 can connect to cloud and edge resources over the internet.

The client libraries rely on an intermediate interface that provides standard functionality to each client library. This library is written in C and is used by all the client libraries, although it is not required for their operation. The middleware abstraction layer, called RMW (ROS Middleware), provides the essential communication interfaces. The vendors for each middleware implement the RMW interface and are made interchangeable without code changes.

Users may choose different RMW implementations, and thereby different middleware technologies, based on various constraints such as performance, software licensing, or supported platforms. The network interfaces (e.g. topics, services, actions) are defined, and ROS 2 defines these types using specific format files.

Communications are agnostic to the location of endpoints within machines and processes. Nodes written as components can be allocated to any process as a configuration, allowing multiple nodes to be configured to share a process, thereby conserving system resources or reducing latency.

1.5 Future Considerations and Research

1.5.1 Deployment Considerations

Autonomous vehicles for last-mile delivery can reshape the final step of the supply chain, from the distribution centre to customers' doorsteps. The primary advantage of autonomous delivery is the potential for significant cost reduction and increased efficiency. These vehicles can operate around the clock, resulting in faster delivery times and improved fleet utilisation. They can also be designed to be more environmentally friendly, contributing to more sustainable logistics practices.

The deployment of unmanned ground and aerial autonomous vehicles and mobile robots requires careful planning and consideration of various factors such as regulatory compliance, integration with existing logistics infrastructure, and public perception. Addressing these factors is essential for the successful adoption of autonomous delivery vehicles in urban areas. Partnerships with local governments and logistics providers can facilitate smoother integration and expansion of services.

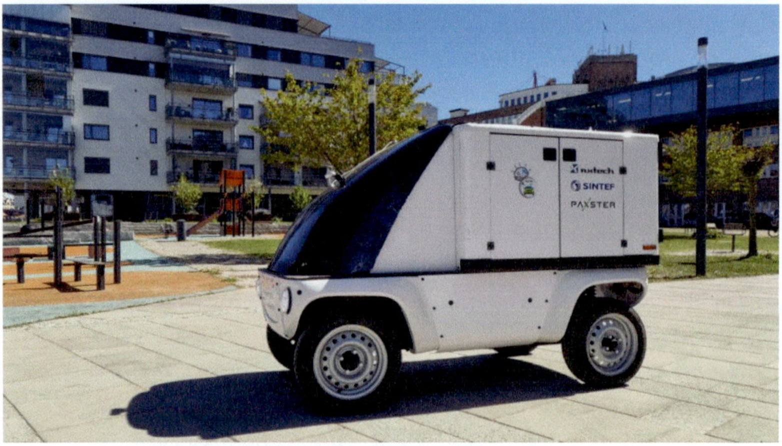

Figure 1.15 The autonomous vehicle [10].

The success of the technology depends on navigating complex urban environments, which include everything from busy streets to unpredictable behaviour of pedestrians and traffic participants.

The path to widespread adoption of last-mile delivery autonomous vehicles is filled with challenges. The technology is still evolving, and ensuring the safety and reliability of autonomous systems is a top priority as the vehicles must be able to navigate a wide range of real-world scenarios, from inclement weather to unexpected road closures.

Public acceptance and the impact on the workforce are also critical considerations. Gaining the trust of consumers and integrating these vehicles into daily life without causing disruption is key.

Generative AI can enhance the interaction between autonomous vehicles and users through natural language processing, allowing users to communicate with delivery systems using voice commands, while facilitating seamless user experiences where customers can track orders or interact directly with service interfaces.

Addressing future trends and overcoming technological, regulatory, and social challenges, while developing new technologies and AI-assisted tools, is key to unlocking the full potential of autonomous last-mile delivery.

1.5.2 Future research

Autonomous last-mile delivery applications are leveraging advancements in edge AI platforms and sensor fusion technologies (camera, LiDAR, IMU, ultrasound, V2X, etc.), specifically tailored to meet the unique requirements and constraints of these applications, including close-quarters navigation, interaction with VRUs, and severe cost and power limitations.

Key architectural concepts, including various levels and strategies for sensor fusion, are employed alongside enabling algorithms (e.g., deep learning methods such as CNNs and Transformers) and hardware components (e.g., GPUs, specialised accelerators, and edge computing platforms). Significant integration challenges, encompassing sensor calibration, data synchronisation, computational load management, power consumption, cost-effectiveness, and fault tolerance, still need to be addressed.

The pressing research challenges are achieving robust perception in adverse conditions, reliable VRU detection, handling sensor limitations, and ensuring the safety and validation of autonomous systems.

Key future research directions include novel fusion architectures, end-to-end learning, self-supervised methods, enhanced V2X integration, explainable edge AI (XAI) and interpretable edge AI (IAI) for fusion, lightweight models for edge deployment, and advanced simulation for validation, all aimed at advancing the safety, reliability, and efficiency of autonomous last-mile delivery.

Future work includes the concept for a dedicated architecture and a multimodal AI-based autonomous vehicle platform for perception, automated control, and decision-making in delivering goods in controlled environments. The work addresses evaluating the integration of data from multiple sensors. Multimodal AI and generative AI enable real-time correlation and a more comprehensive understanding of the vehicle's surroundings, allowing for vehicle control through voice and gesture commands.

Future work plans to address the adoption of new concepts provided by Software-Defined and AI-Defined Vehicles (SDV/AIDV) architectures, where the vehicle's features and functionality are determined by the holistic interplay between sensors/actuators, the hardware, software, AI platforms, and data and ROS is well-suited to this new paradigm, as it provides a flexible and modular platform for developing and deploying a wide range of applications.

As last-mile delivery autonomous vehicles operate in fleets and are connected, there is a growing trend towards offloading the computational tasks to the edge. ROS 2's support for DDS makes it easy to extend the vehicle's communication system to include edge-based services.

Further research is addressing the advancements of autonomous delivery vehicles, focusing on enhancing the human-machine interfaces between

[20] Z. Feng, "Application and Development of Radar Sensors in Autonomous Driving Technology," Applied and Computational Engineering, Vol. 140, No. 1, pp. 48–52, Mar. 2025, doi: https://doi.org/10.54254/2755-2721/2025.21277.

[21] HESAI, "The Role of Lidar in the Future of Autonomous Vehicles," *HESAI*, Jun. 12, 2023. https://www.hesaitech.com/the-role-of-lidar-in-the-future-of-autonomous-vehicles/.

[22] A. Singh, "Transformer-Based Sensor Fusion for Autonomous Driving: A Survey," 2023 IEEE/CVF International Conference on Computer Vision Workshops (ICCVW), Paris, France, 2023, pp. 3304-3309, https://www.doi.org/10.1109/ICCVW60793.2023.00355.

[23] G. Mittermaier. "How important are sensors for autonomous vehicles?," Md-elektronik.com, Apr. 25, 2025. https://www.md-elektronik.com/en/how-important-are-sensors-for-autonomous-vehicles/

[24] Fiveable, "Inertial measurement units (IMU)", Autonomous Vehicle Systems Class Notes, Fiveable, 2024. https://library.fiveable.me/autonomous-vehicle-systems/unit-2/inertial-measurement-units-imu/study-guide/ff0fWwVL7g5SSoEF

[25] JOUAV, "A Complete Guide to Inertial Measurement Unit (IMU)," *JOUAV*, 2025. https://www.jouav.com/blog/inertial-measurement-unit.html

[26] Leadvent Group, "The Essential Role of Sensor Accuracy in Autonomous Vehicle Safety," *Leadventgrp.com*, Sep. 10, 2024. https://www.leadventgrp.com/blog/the-role-of-sensor-accuracy-in-ensuring-av-safety

[27] Fiveable "Ultrasonic sensors", Autonomous Vehicle Systems Class Notes, Fiveable 2024. https://library.fiveable.me/autonomous-vehicle-systems/unit-2/ultrasonic-sensors/study-guide/uTe34rwjgIartZFT

[28] Caradas, "Ultrasonic Sensors in Cars" *Caradas*, Dec. 02, 2023. https://caradas.com/understanding-ultrasonic-sensors-in-cars/

[29] G. Sankar, "How embedded vision is transforming last mile delivery with delivery robots," *e-con Systems*, Oct. 26, 2022. https://www.e-consystems.com/blog/camera/applications/autonomous-mobile-robots-amr/how-embedded-vision-is-transforming-last-mile-delivery-with-delivery-robots/

[30] T. Huang *et al.*, "V2X Cooperative Perception for Autonomous Driving: Recent Advances and Challenges," *arXiv.org*, Nov. 06, 2023. https://arxiv.org/abs/2310.03525

[31] Y. He, B. Wu, Z. Dong, J. Wan and W. Shi, "Towards C-V2X Enabled Collaborative Autonomous Driving," in IEEE Transactions on Vehicular Technology, vol. 72, no. 12, pp. 15450-15462, Dec. 2023, https://www.doi.org/10.1109/TVT.2023.3299844.

[32] S. Raghavan, B. Pistone, D. Gibb, J. Gasser, N. Pednekar, and S. Marzani, "Software-defined Vehicles, GenAI, IoT – The Path to AI-Defined Vehicles, Amazon Web Services," *Amazon Web Services*, Mar. 13, 2025. https://aws.amazon.com/blogs/industries/software-defined-vehicles-genai-iot-the-path-to-ai-defined-vehicles/.

[33] S. Gajendra, "What are AI-Defined Vehicles and Why They Are the Future of Automotive?" Arm Newsroom, May 28, 2025. https://newsroom.arm.com/blog/what-are-ai-defined-vehicles.

[34] A. Jose and B. Daniel, "Reimagining / Redefining SDVs: Embracing the AI-Defined Vehicle Era," Frost & Sullivan, Jun. 10, 2024. https://www.frost.com/growth-opportunity-news/reimagining-redefining-sdvs-embracing-the-ai-defined-vehicle-era/.

[35] P. Estefo, J. Simmonds, R. Robbes, and J. Fabry, "The Robot Operating System: Package reuse and community dynamics," Journal of Systems and Software, vol. 151, pp. 226–242, May 2019, https://doi.org/10.1016/j.jss.2019.02.024.

[36] M. Martínez-Díaz, C. Al-Haddad, F. Soriguera, and C. Antoniou, "Platooning of connected automated vehicles on freeways: a bird's eye view," Transportation Research Procedia, vol. 58, pp. 479–486, Jan. 2021, https://doi.org/10.1016/j.trpro.2021.11.064.

[37] O. Vermesan et al., "Automotive Intelligence Embedded in Electric Connected Autonomous and Shared Vehicles Technology for Sustainable Green Mobility," Frontiers in Future Transportation, vol. 2, Aug. 2021, https://doi.org/10.3389/ffutr.2021.688482.

[38] G. Jocher, "ultralytics/yolov5," GitHub, Aug. 21, 2020. https://github.com/ultralytics/yolov5

[39] G. Jocher, A. Chaurasia, and J. Qiu, "YOLOv8 by Ultralytics," GitHub, 2023. https://github.com/ultralytics/ultralytics

[40] M. Quigley *et al.*, "ROS: an open-source Robot Operating System." Available at: https://robotics.stanford.edu/$~$ang/papers/icraoss09-ROS.pdf.

[41] A. Ademovic, "An Introduction to Robot Operating System: The Ultimate Robot Application Framework," *Toptal Engineering Blog*. https://www.toptal.com/robotics/introduction-to-robot-operating-system.

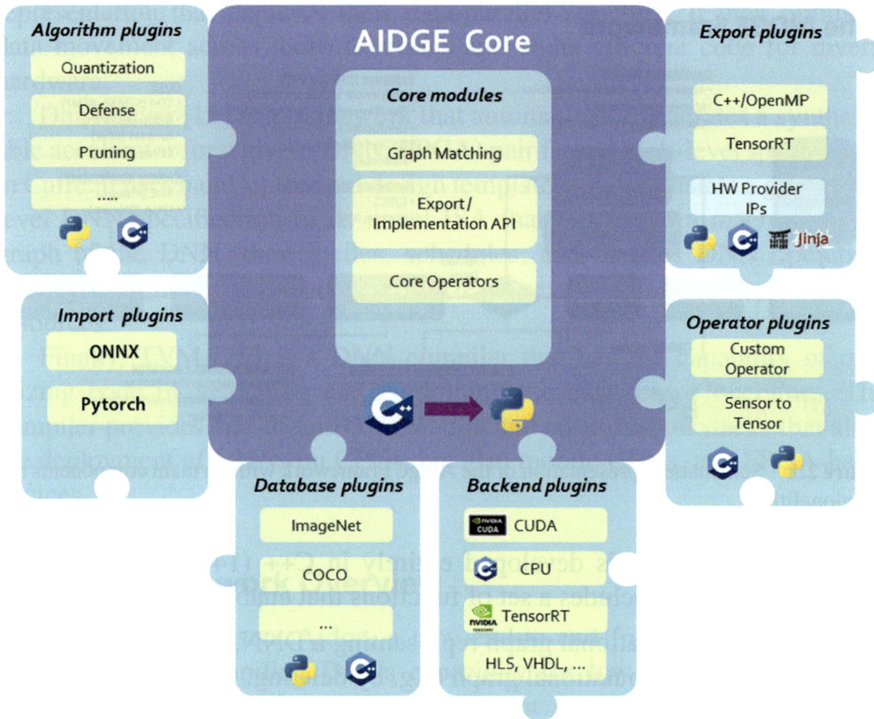

Figure 2.2 Aidge is built upon the concept of modularity with a "Core" component and several "plugins" that complete and extend the framework.

and the library used for the implementation (with its data type and a number precision)

Plugins allow developers and users to add or adapt functionalities of the platform. Different kinds of plugins can be developed (in C++ or Python) using the Aidge API, such as:

- "Recipe plugins", which may allow to load and save the network description in a specific format, or it may consist in a set of optimizer algorithms, for example to reduce the model's cost in terms of memory and computing complexity, or to increase its robustness against external/adversarial attacks.
- "Dataset plugins", which add the capability to load data and labels from a specific dataset.
- "Backend plugins", which register to the Core compiled kernel libraries (e.g. C++, CUDA, HLS) allowing it to execute the computational graph.

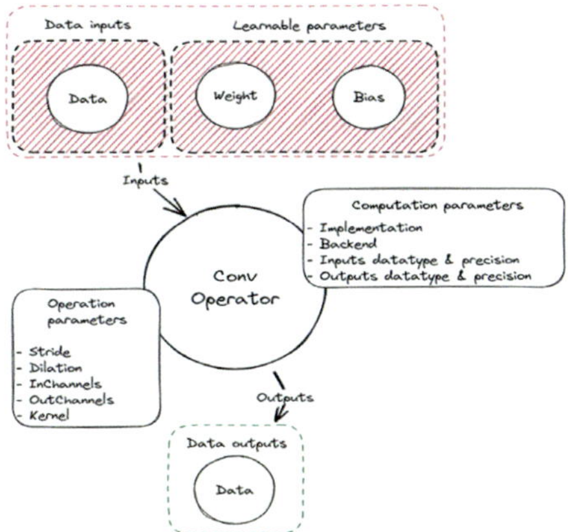

Figure 2.3 The image shows the constituent parts of an example Convolution operator.

- "Operator plugins", which adds the ability to define a new operator in C++ which is not available in the Core.
- "Export plugins", which define a set of rules and methods aimed at adapting the graph to the targeted hardware, and methods to produce source code corresponding to the optimized graph.

2.2.1 Internal Graph Representation

Aidge's low-level architecture is designed to allow the highest flexibility in DNN representation and computation, thus DNN models are represented using a directional "computational graph". This graph is composed of a set of nodes, representing operations (Operators), connected with directed edges, representing the flow of data.

Nodes in this computational graph are defined by three properties: the *connectivity*, the *operation description*, and the *implementation*.

1. Operation description: it describes the operation a node will do (e.g. Convolution, ReLu, Data Provider, etc.) and its attributes (see Figure 2.3). This description is agnostic of the implementation. The attributes are the following:
    - The sizes of the Kernel, Dilation (in case of convolutions), Stride, etc.
    - The number of inputs and their dimensions, datatype and precision;
    - The number of outputs and their dimensions, datatype and precision;

  - A reference to a *forward* (i.e. inference) function implementation;
  - A reference to a *backward* (i.e. train) function implementation.

2. Connectivity: it describes which nodes (proper Operators or Data Providers) are connected to a given node.
3. Implementation: it points to the computational function/kernel used by the Operator for its forward and backward operations. The selection of the right implementation is made via a *registrar system* depending on the following attributes:
   - The Backend, defined by both the hardware target (e.g. CPU, GPU, ...) and available libraries (e.g OpenCV)
   - The DataType (float, int, ...) and Precision (8bits, 16bits, 32bits,...) of the inputs and outputs
   - The DataFormat (NCHW, NHWC, ...)
   - The Kernel, the algorithm chosen to perform the computation

This flexible computational graph description is paired with the ability to use a great variety of data representation (e.g. Tensors, Sparse Tensors, Event Based stimuli, etc.).

2.2.2 Platform interoperability

Thanks to PyBind11, there is a seamless interoperability with Numpy arrays, achieved by defining a *buffer_protocol* in the binding of Aidge Tensors. This allows to use data imported from other frameworks that are compatible with Numpy.

Aidge is interoperable with PyTorch and allows:

- Creating an Aidge Tensor from a PyTorch Tensor
- Running an Aidge (sub)graph within the PyTorch environment.
- Running an Aidge computational graph within the PyTorch environment.

Aidge allows interoperability with Keras by creating a wrapper from a Keras Model through a conversion step via an ONNX file.

Similarly to PyTorch, Aidge can convert Keras tensors by using the Numpy interoperability.

2.2.3 Graph Regular Expression (GraphRegex)

The proposed Aidge's internal graph representation is a powerful tool that combines carefully chosen abstraction levels. The strategy is to adapt the internal representation to narrow the gap between a neural network and hardware devices. Aidge proposes an innovative way to facilitate the manipulation of the internal graph representation: the Graph Regular Expression or GraphRegex

The Graph Regular Expression combines two main innovations:

1. A description of graph patterns. Taking inspiration from regular expressions from the formal language theory, we introduce a new language to describe a set of graphs starting from a sequence of characters.
2. Graph matching. Aidge provides a function that allows to extract a subset of the graph matching the provided GraphRegex description.

Graph Regular Expression is complementary to other graph transformation methods such as adding and removing nodes or entire parts of the graph.

With GraphRegex it is possible to work on two distinct levels in a graph:

1. At a conditional level, which corresponds to checking the presence of a node in a defined dictionary.
2. At a topological level, which allows to describe the interconnections between symbols.

The topological description, can be compared to classical regular expressions, as it is a form of symbol sequence expression, but extended to the definition of graphs.

At a practical level, this matching method can be subdivided into two distinct stages. First, we describe the desired pattern with the syntax of regular expressions, then we search for that pattern inside the graphs. These two steps together form the GraphRegex Query.

After extracting all the subgraphs corresponding to a GraphRegex Query, it is possible to use an intersection resolution algorithm to obtain intersection-free solutions. However, it is important to note that these algorithms can have a high complexity, which can make their execution time-consuming.

2.2.4 Network optimization

We can define two categories of optimizations: topological ones, which change the structure of the computation graph, and parametrical ones, which change the parameters of the nodes.

An example of topological modification is Tiling. This method splits convolutions in several ones (for example in 4 convolutions, as show in Figure 2.4). All of them are computed independently and concatenated at the end. This manipulation is mathematically exact (lossless).

Here is the practical implementation:

```
import aidge_core
import aidge_backend_cpu
import aidge_onnx
import numpy as np
#  Let's create a small neural network with four layers.
model = aidge_core.sequential([ aidge_core.LeakyReLU(1,
    name= "leakyrelu0" ), aidge_core.Conv2D(3, 32, [3, 3],
    name="conv0"), aidge_core.BatchNorm2D(32, name="bn0"),
    aidge_core.ReLU( name="relu0" ) ])
tiled_conv = aidge_core.get_conv_horizontal_tiling(
    model.get_node("conv0"), 2, 4)
node_to_replace = {model.get_node("conv0"),
    model.get_node("conv0").get_parent(1),
    model.get_node("conv0").get_parent(2)}
aidge_core.GraphView.replace(node_to_replace, tiled_conv)
```

Figure 2.4 Example of operator tiling/splitting: a Conv + Relu subgraph is split into a Slice + 4 Conv + 4 Relu + Concat.

One of the key differentiators compared to other frameworks such as LLVM, is that Aidge applies directly graph modifications, which allows to make global topological changes as opposed to only focus on local ones.

On the other hand, an example of parametrical optimization is quantization after training (PTQ) or during training (QAT). This is a well-established method for reducing memory usage and in most cases, accelerating the inference. PTQ is very useful when one does not have the time or the possibility to re-run the training and does not need to quantize to more than to 8-bits. If fewer bits are necessary, state-of-the-art QAT methods give very good results. These and other techniques (e.g. LSQ and FracBit QAT) are currently being finalized in Aidge.

2.2.5 Export phase

One of the aims of Aidge is to produce an interpretable, explainable and auditable output. To do this Aidge produces/exports source code files and a number of related resource files that form a complete package.

In Figure 2.5, which summarizes the export strategy, it is possible to see two phases: Export Mapping and Export Implementation.

The first objective of the Export Mapping phase is to modify the computational graph to fit the target hardware by using several optimization techniques (e.g. hardware mapping optimization or graph transformation).

The second objective is the generation of the graph scheduling constrained by the architecture rules of the target and additional project rules imposed by the developer or the user (e.g. the available memory, the available computer resources or the time allocated for the execution).

Taking into account the architecture rules and the project constraints, the scheduler will generate a sequential list of nodes from the optimized graph that will determine how the forward process (i.e. the inference) of the exported DNN will run on the target.

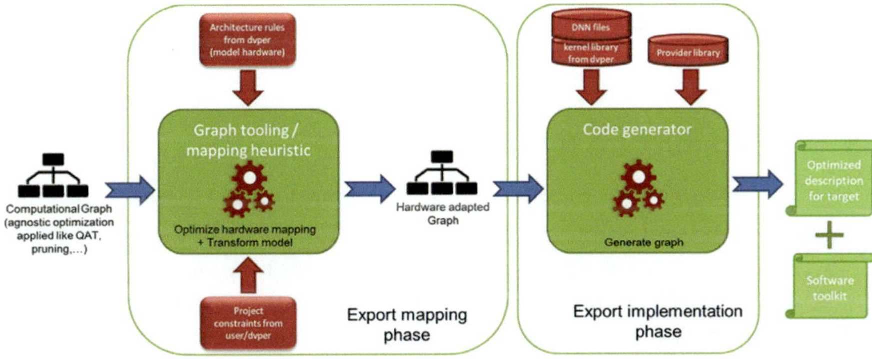

Figure 2.5 Schematic representation of Aidge's export procedure.

The Export Implementation phase aims at producing a source code of the hardware-tuned graph returned by the scheduler. The typical steps for generating source code are the following:

1. Design and export the computation kernels.
2. Export the attributes of the nodes.
3. Export the parameters of the nodes.

Each node of the graph must have an implementation of its forward method in order to use it in the export. Since only the hardware developers really know the characteristics and capabilities of their devices, it is their duty to provide the implementations of the computation kernels. These may be implemented as a kernel library, which is a collection of optimized functions developed by expert programmers targeting the architecture (computing functions, DMA programming, etc...).

Together with the kernels, Aidge generates the configuration and parameter files, and also the files that contain the source code of the forward function of the hardware-adapted graph.

The developer has also the possibility to add files to generate a whole Software Toolkit that will provide functionalities such as:

- Compilation or project files to compile the export
- Files to run a whole application of the export
- Set of unitary tests (to test the kernels on board, ...)
- Input data for tests
- Third party libraries to use board functions
- Resources to check other constraints like security rules or robustness directives
- Memory map files indicating information about the static allocation of the resources used by the

2.3 Conclusion and future work

In this article we proposed Aidge, a framework that allows end-to-end manipulation, optimization and compilation of DNN architectures and their deployment to a vast spectrum of hardware devices ranging CPUs to GPUs, MCUs, DSPs, FPGAs and neuromorphic architectures. Another aim of this framework is to develop and provide reusable hardware building blocks and methodologies that are transversal to all types of architectures.

We would like to point out that one of the driving motivations for the development of this framework was the need to answer industrial challenges for the usability of AI.

For what concerns future work we foresee the extension of the number of target architectures including low power ASICS such as PNeuro [17], STM32, NeuroCorgi [18] and RISC-V.

Moreover, we will focus on graph optimization developing methods for Quantization Aware Training (QAT), Mixed Precision Quantization, Compression, Pruning, and Spike coding.

We also plan to add a greater number of supported functionalities and models such as: Object Detectors, Semantic Segmentation, Multimodal fusion, Attention models (Transformers)

Finally, we will start to tackle on-chip learning capabilities.

The framework is under active development using an open source and collaborative process and can be found at:

projects.eclipse.org/projects/technology.aidge

and

https://eclipse-aidge.readthedocs.io/en/latest/

Acknowledgements

We would like to thank the members of the Aidge development group for their work on the framework and for their valuable contributions to this paper.

This work was supported in part by the Neurokit2E European Project (GA101112268), and the DeepGreen Projet (ANR-23-DEGR-0001).

References

[1] N. P. Jouppi, et al., "In-datacenter performance analysis of a tensor processing," in *Proceedings of the 44th Annual International Symposium*, New York, 2017.

[2] M. Abadi, et al., "Tensorflow: A system for large-scale machine learning," in *12th USENIX Symposium on Operating Systems Design and Implementation*, p. 265–283, 2016.

[3] A. Paszk, et al., "PyTorch: An Imperative Style, High-Performance Deep Learning Library," ArXiv, 2019.

[4] J. Bai, F. Lu, K. Zhang et al., "ONNX: Open Neural Network Exchange," 2019, https://github.com/onnx/onnx

[5] Y.-H. Chen, J. Emer and V. Sze, "Eyeriss: A spatial architecture for energy-efficient dataflow for convolutional neural networks," in *Proceedings of the 43rd International Symposium on Computer Architecture (ISCA '16)*, New York, 2016.

[6] Y. Chen, T. Luo, S. Liu et al., "Dadiannao: A machine-learning supercomputer," in *Proceedings of the 47th Annual IEEE/ACM International Symposium on Microarchitecture*, p. 609–622, 2014.

[7] NVIDIA, "H100 Tensor Core GPU," 2023, https://www.nvidia.com/en-us/data-center/h100/

[8] NVIDIA, "Grace CPU," 2023, https://www.nvidia.com/en-us/data-center/grace-cpu/

[9] NVIDIA, "Hopper CPU," 2023, https://www.nvidia.com/en-us/data-center/technologies/hopper-architecture/

[10] Intel, "Intel Core Processor Family," 2023, https://www.intel.com/content/www/us/en/products/details/processors/core.html

[11] R. Wei, V. Adve and R. Schwartz, "DLVM: A modern compiler infrastructure for deep learning systems," ArXiv, 2017.

[12] N. Rotem, et al., "Glow: Graph Lowering Compiler Techniques for Neural Networks," arXiv, 2019.

[13] J. Ragan-Kelley, C. Barnes, S. Adams et al., "Halide: A language and compiler for optimizing parallelism, locality, and recomputation in image processing pipelines," Proceedings of the 34th ACM SIGPLAN Conference on Programming Language Design and Implementation, pp. 519-530, 2013.

[14] S. Palkar, J. J. Thomas, D. Narayana et al., "Weld: Rethinking the interface between data-intensive applications," ArXiv, 2017.

[15] H. Sharma, J. Park, D. Mahajan et al., "From High-Level Deep Neural Models to FPGAs," "49th Annual IEEE/ACM International Symposium on Microarchitecture", pp. 1-12, 2016.

[16] T. Chen, T. Moreau, Z. Jiang et al., "TVM: An automated end-to-end optimizing compiler for deep learning," In 13th USENIX Symposium on Operating Systems Design and Implementation, p. 578–594, 2018.

[17] A. Carbon, J. M. Philippe, O. Bichler and et al., "PNeuro: a scalable energy-efficient programmable hardware accelerator for neural networks," Design, Automation & Test in Europe Conference & Exhibition, 2018.

[18] CEA-List, "NeuroCorgi," 2023, https://github.com/CEA-LIST/neurocorgi_sdk.

3

A scalable and flexible interconnect-based dataflow architecture for Edge AI Inference

Rohit Prasad and Hana Krichene

Université Paris-Saclay, CEA-List, France

Abstract

The scalable approach of edge artificial intelligence (AI) inference, especially Convolutional Neural Network (CNN) for computer vision and image recognition functions, has increased its computational complexity due to the involvement of multiple properties, i.e., input image size, choice of the filter size, zero padding, and strides. Dataflow architectures based on many Processing Elements (PEs) are considered promising solutions to execute CNNs, efficiently offering high parallelism and bandwidth. However, the existing dataflow architectures are generally specialised with difficulty in achieving scalability and flexibility. This work proposes an interconnect-based dataflow architecture to overcome such problems. The proposed architecture can efficiently handle convolutions featuring different input image/feature-map shapes and filters, with data reuse and communication-computation overlap. It is scalable and configurable to adapt to different CNN layers. The experimental results show that the proposed architecture can accelerate LeNet5 convolution layers by up to 71.2× in latency performance w.r.t. a RISC-V-based CPU and that it also accelerates MobileNetV2 convolution layers by up to 2.07× in latency performance w.r.t. a dataflow architecture featuring row-stationary execution style.

Keywords: dataflow architecture, data reuse, CNN accelerator, interconnect, hardware accelerator.

DOI: 10.1201/9788743808633-3

3.1 Introduction

CNNs used for Deep Learning (DL) are increasingly achieving higher accuracy in processing modern Artificial Intelligence (AI) applications such as computer vision [4] and image recognition [6]. Existing CNNs face problems of high computational complexity and large amounts of data to process. The problem becomes more critical in the context of Edge AI due to the availability of limited resources. Dataflow architectures [10] are presented as a promising solution to provide high parallelism with high throughput while facilitating the movement of shared data via Network-on-Chip (NoC). These architectures are based on massive PEs performing an elementary function, e.g., Multiply-ACcumulate (MAC) operation in the case of CNN processing. Due to the large amount of data in CNN processing, NoC [8] ensures data exchange among PEs, and between PEs and memories. On the one hand, existing dataflow architectures are specialised and not very flexible for a given CNN. Ensuring the flexibility of the architecture and data transfer with the least delay without compromising the computation are the keys to improving the performance of those dataflow architectures.

We propose an interconnect-based dataflow architecture in this work. The proposed architecture comprises distributed memories and an array of PEs interconnected via a mesh interconnect network. The underlying interconnect network provides high bandwidth and injection rate to achieve simultaneous data transfers via parallel routing paths. The interconnect network also provides flexible data transfers with different directions of multicast and broadcast. Thanks to this interconnect network, the proposed architecture can scale and fit the ever-increasing size of ever-evolving neural networks and accommodate the amount of data generated. The employed interconnect network is configurable, allowing the proposed architecture to handle different CNN shapes and layers of shapes of the same CNN and optimise the PE utilisation by generating a suitable design configuration for a given convolution processing. This benefits the proposed architecture to maximise the reuse of shared data and the communication-computation overlap.

The remainder of the paper is organised as follows, section 1.2 discusses the related work, section 1.3 presents the background work, section 1.4 describes the sub-system of the proposed architecture, section 1.5 explains the execution model of the proposed architecture, section 1.6 presents the evaluation methodology, details the experiments, and analyses the performance results. Finally, section 1.7 presents a conclusion.

3.2 Related Work

Typically, in dataflow architecture, a program is seen as a collection of data nodes where a data flow node is executed when all its inputs are ready. Once a result is ready at a data node, copies of the result are distributed to their destination operators. This chain of operations is performed in sequential order until the end of execution of the program is reached. There is no separate control flow, and operations scheduling requires in-depth knowledge of the underlying algorithm of the program. The scope of this section is limited to the dataflow architectures that target the acceleration of CNNs only.

In [16], a dataflow architecture called Eyeriss is presented that aims to save energy consumption by minimising the data movement on a PE array. Eyeriss exploits the reuse of filter weights and feature map pixels in the convolutions to minimise the data movement due to the accumulations of partial sums. Eyeriss limits the dimensions of input data due to its fixed PE array size.

The DianNao series, i.e., DianNao [13], DaDianNao [14], and ShiDianNao [19] aim to increase the efficiency of the system by minimising the latency of memory accesses. DaDianNao minimises the main-memory access latency by implementing a large on-chip embedded Dynamic Random Access Memory (eDRAM). DaDianNao is targeted at the data center solution. ShiDianNao targets the acceleration of CNN applications by mapping the parameters onto a smaller on-chip Static Random Access Memory (SRAM). ShiDianNao has a better energy efficiency than DaDianNao by 60$\times$ because the former avoids memory access to DRAM by storing data in SRAM.

Maeri [7] is another dataflow architecture that augments multiplication and addition operators with tiny switches, and communication is available to them using a reconfigurable interconnect network. Maeri can execute convolution, Long Short-Term Memory (LSTM), pooling, and fully connected layers. It supports cross-layer mapping and also addresses sparsity in the network.

These architectures feature a different approach for mapping and executing convolution layers. In addition to these architectures, the proposed architecture features the overlap between communication and computation, and a scalable PE array to adapt to different input data sizes.

3.3 Background: dataflow execution models

In DNN, the same data is used at multiple input data locations. If repeated accesses of the temporal data from memory are performed, such repetition can degrade the performance of a sub-system in terms of latency and energy consumption. Dataflow architectures can stand out in such situations because these architectures can efficiently exploit data reuse to avoid repeated memory accesses of temporal data. There are four ways dataflow architectures exploit data reuse, which is defined in the existing convolution neural networks, i.e., (1) Weight Stationary (WS), (2) Input Stationary (IS), (3) Output Stationary (OS), and (4) Row Stationary (RS). Below is a short description of each dataflow model:

1. *WS dataflow model* exploits the filter weight data reuse. NeuFlow [3] implements such a dataflow model.
2. *IS dataflow model* exploits the data reuse by distributing image/input feature maps (ifmaps) to multiple processing elements (PEs). SCNN [1] implements such a strategy to handle sparse CNNs, where multiple filter weight data are zeros.
3. *OS dataflow model* exploits data reuse by broadcasting filter weights, and ifmaps are reused throughout the PE array. ShiDianNao [19] implements such a strategy, where each PE produces the outputs by sharing ifmap data from the neighbouring PEs.
4. *RS dataflow model* reuses ifmaps, filter, and partial sum (intermediate result) to accelerate convolutions. Eyeriss [15] implements such a strategy. Data reuse is performed by sending filter data horizontally and ifmap data diagonally. Once all the PEs in the array have received their respective data, execution begins. Partial sums are accumulated by moving them vertically in each PE column. The dimension of the PE array is determined by filter size and output feature map (ofmap) size for a particular layer. The proposed architecture also uses the RS dataflow model to exploit data reuse in the execution of convolutions.

3.4 Interconnect-based dataflow architecture

Figure 3.1 (a) represents the proposed architecture, which includes (1) a Neural Global Controller (NGC), (2) a Neural Processing Element (NPE) array connected through (3) an Artificial Intelligence Network on Chip (AINoC), and (4) Global Buffers (GB) for storing input and output data. The rows of the filter and rows of the ofmap determine the size of the NPE array, e.g. if the filter size is 6×6, then the number of rows in the NPE array would be 6, and the number of columns would be equal to the number of rows in ofmap, which is computed using the equation below:

$$ofmap\_rows = (((ifmaps\_rows - (filter\_rows + padding\_start + padding\_end))/stride) + 1)$$

3.4.1 NGC: Neural Global Controller

The NGC is a five-stage Finite-State Machine (FSM) shown in Figure 3.1 (b). Following is the description of each stage:

1. *IDLE* represents the idle state of the NGC.
2. *LOAD_config* loads and decodes the configuration line for the current layer, including the size and number of filters and ifmaps for the current layer.
3. *LOAD_filter* starts sending the filter data (i.e., payload) and the control word from the Input GBs (IGBs) to the connected routers. Depending on the opcode, routers either unicast, multicast, or broadcast the incoming payload data to the AINoC.
4. *LOAD_ifmaps* starts sending the ifmaps data and the control word from the IGBs to the connected router. Depending on the opcode, routers either unicast, multicast, or broadcast the incoming payload data to the AINoC. LOAD_filter and LOAD_ifmaps states can be interchanged to provide some flexibility in the data loading order in the proposed architecture.
5. *COMPUTE* starts the MAC operations in the NPEs. Once a Partial Sum (PSum) is computed in the bottom row NPEs, the results are sent to their respective north NPEs along with their control words. The NPEs in the upper row then add the incoming results with their locally computed PSum and send the computed result to their north NPEs. This chain of operations is executed until it reaches the top NPE row, where the final PSum is stored in the Output GBs (OGBs) to be used in the next layer.

3.4.2 NPE: Neural Processing Element

The NPE is a simple operator controlled by the FSM of the NGC, as shown in Figure 3.1 (c). It remains in the idle state until the NGC triggers the execution. It proceeds in this way according to the control signals sent by the NGC:

- When the load_filter signal is received, it stores the incoming payload into the filter Register File (RF). Once all the NPEs have received their corresponding filter data, the top right NPE in the NPE array sends a signal to NGC to jump to the next state.

- When the load_ifmap signal is received, it stores the incoming payload into the ifmaps RF. Once all the NPEs have received their corresponding ifmaps data, the top right NPE in the NPE array sends a signal to NGC to jump to the next state.

When the start_compute signal is received, it begins the MAC operation on the filter and ifmaps data and generates PSum. Then, it either (i) sends the PSum to the north NPE (if bottom row NPE) or (ii) adds the incoming PSum from the south NPE with local PSum and sends the result to the north NPE or OGB (if top row NPE). In this phase, communication-computation overlap is also performed by the NPEs, which received their required data.

At the end of the computation, an end_compute signal will be sent by the last NPE of the array to inform the NGC of the end of the execution, in order to move on to the next execution and the loading of new data.

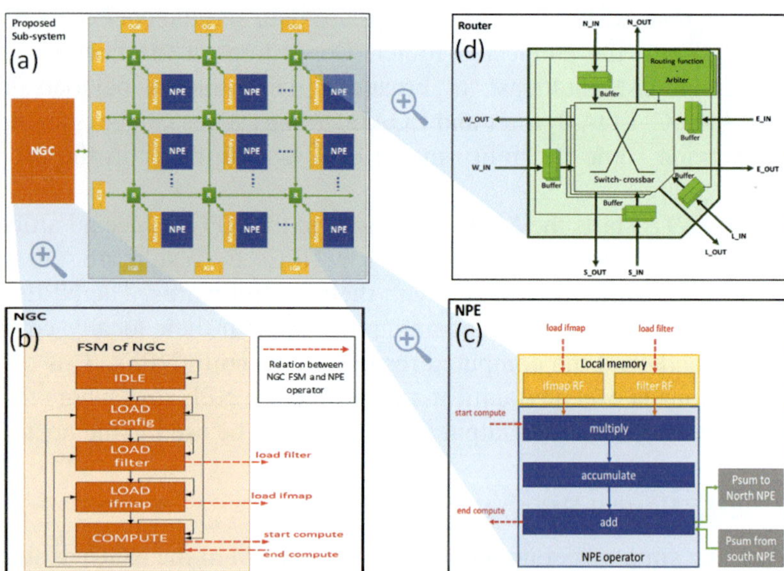

Figure 3.1 (a) The proposed interconnect-based dataflow architecture sub-system, (b) Neural Global Controller (NGC), (c) Neural Processing Element (NPE), (d) Router in Artificial Intelligence Network on Chip (AINoC).

3.4.3 AINoC: Artificial Intelligence Network-on-Chip

The AINoC [9] consists of routers optimised for parallel dataflow processing with minimal data transfer cost to achieve energy-efficient CNN processing without compromising accuracy and application performance.

As shown in Figure 3.1 (d), the routing device is composed of several parallel routing paths, each including a buffer, a communication controller, an arbiter, and a switch. All these paths are designed to guarantee a large bandwidth and flexible communication. Indeed, through several buffering modules, e.g. First-In-First-Out (FIFO), different communication requests received in parallel can be stored without any loss. These requests are then processed simultaneously in several control modules. These modules ensure a deterministic control of the data transfer according to a static X-Y (X-direction priority) routing algorithm and management of different communications (unicast, multicast, and broadcast). Parallel arbitration of the processing order of incoming data packets according to the Round-Robin Arbitration (RRA) [5] based on scheduled access allows for better collision management, i.e., a request that has just been granted, will have the lowest priority on the next arbitration cycle. Parallel switching comes next to simultaneously route data to the right outputs according to the Wormhole switching [11], i.e. the connection between one of the inputs and one of the outputs of a router is maintained until all the elementary data of a message packet are sent and this in a simultaneous way through the different switching modules.

The data packet format is shown in Figure 3.2. A data message consists of two packets: a control packet followed by a data packet. A packet is composed of a header (flit code) and a payload. In the control packet, the payload is a destination or source address, while in the data packet, the payload is a set of data flits. The packet size is 32-bit. However, the size of the header and the payload are variable. It depends on the size of the interconnection network, as the number of routing devices increases, more bits are needed to encode the addresses of the receivers or senders. Similarly, the flit size and number vary with the size of the payloads (filter weights, activation inputs, or PSums) to be passed through the network. The value of the header determines the communication to be provided by the router. There are three possible types of communication inter-PEs: unicast, multicast (horizontal, vertical, and diagonal), and broadcast. For memory access, the

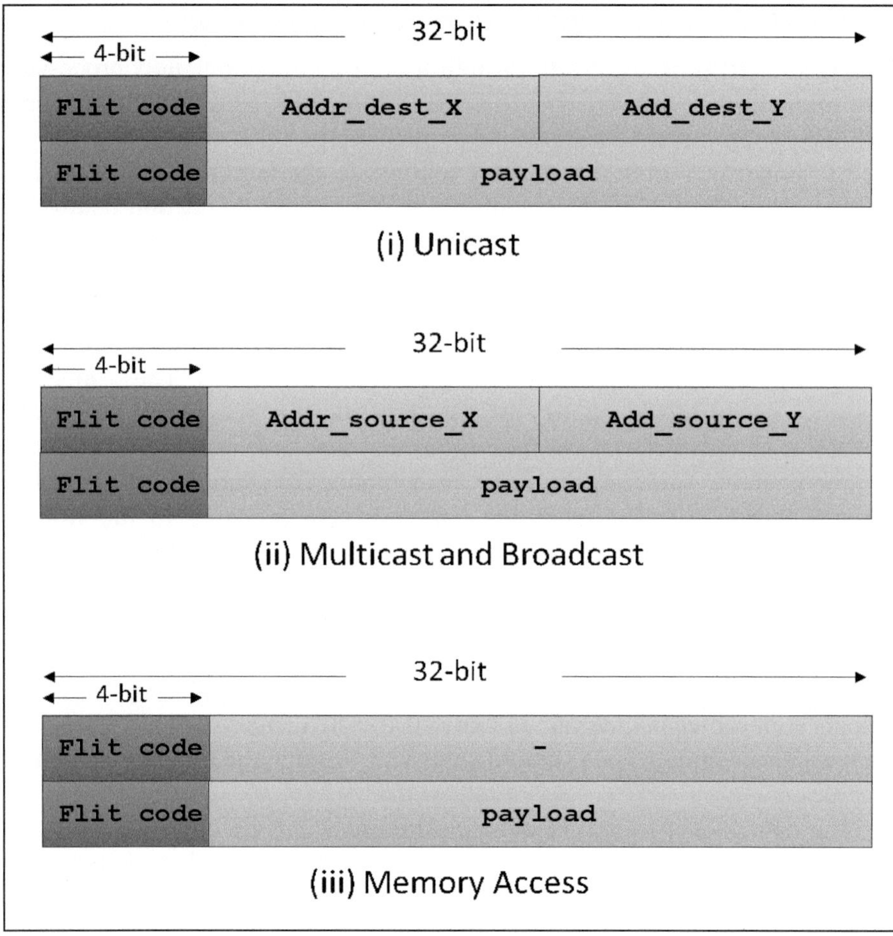

Figure 3.2 Packet format

reading from the IGB is a multicast communication; however, the writing to the OGB is a communication type that processes a direct parallel unicast from the first NPEs rows, and the OGB. The routing device first receives the control packet containing the type of communication and the source or destination address. The routing device decodes this control packet and then allocates the communication path to transmit the data packet that arrives at the cycle following the control packet. Once the data flits are transmitted, the allocated path will be released for further transfers.

3.4.4 Global Buffers

GBs are dual-port Random Access Memory (DPRAM) that are used to store the input data i.e., filter and ifmaps or output data i.e., PSum from top row NPEs. The size of each GB type is determined according to the data size requirement for each layer, such that the overhead due to GB is minimised.

3.5 Execution Model

The data movement and execution pattern in the proposed architecture are presented in this section. Once the data is ready in IGB, the execution in the proposed architecture can be divided into three phases, i.e., (1) load ifmap data into their respective NPEs, (2) load filter data into their respective NPEs, and (3) perform execution on the available data in each NPE. These steps are explained below:

1. *Load ifmap data*: In this phase, ifmap data are loaded into their respective NPEs. Data from IGBs are diagonally loaded into the NPEs, which have connections with them through a single router, and then data reuse is performed by moving the data diagonally to the target NPEs.
2. *Load filter data*: In this phase, filter data are loaded into their respective PEs. Data from IGBs are horizontally loaded into the NPEs, which have connections with them through a single router, and then data reuse is performed by moving the data horizontally to their respective NPEs. During this phase, the overlap between communication and computation is also performed. The NPEs, which receive the required data to compute the partial sum, begin the computation phase. Particularly, the first column of the NPE array gets all the required data and jumps from the communication (i.e., data receiving) phase to the computation phase while other columns still wait for input data.
3. *Execute MAC operation*: When an NPE receives all required data, it jumps from the communication phase to the computation phase. Each column is locally synchronised, where the bottom NPE sends the computed PSum to the north NPE. Each NPE (except the bottom NPE) adds the PSum received from their south NPE with the locally computed PSum before sending the result to their north NPE. This chain of receiving, adding, and sending data is performed until the data reaches the top NPE, where the computed result is stored back into the OGB. NPE array is executing in the Globally Asynchronous Locally

grid of computing elements to process large convolution layers. For the GB memories, we opted for the use of Block Random Access Memory (BRAM) by forcing the synthesis tool to choose these memory blocks instead of the configurable logic blocks (CLB). We also notice that the size of the router is relatively larger than the NPE. This can be explained by NPE providing a simple convolution operation. At the same time, the router has multiple routing paths to provide parallel multicast and control of blocking areas in the communication network. These multiple routing paths mainly accelerate the data transfer and reduce the energy consumption during the execution of a convolution layer. It is then a trade-off between area and performance in the proposed architecture. Area can be treated as a small overhead to ensure a balance in the choice of the architecture and the objectives to be achieved.

Table 3.2 Breakdown of Versal ACAP VCK190 FPGA resources used by the modules of the proposed architecture after synthesis

Module	CLB	BRAM	Area occupancy (%)
NGC	12.21	0	0.02
GB	0	0.5	0.05
Router	76.78	0	0.13
NPE	39.10	0	0.07

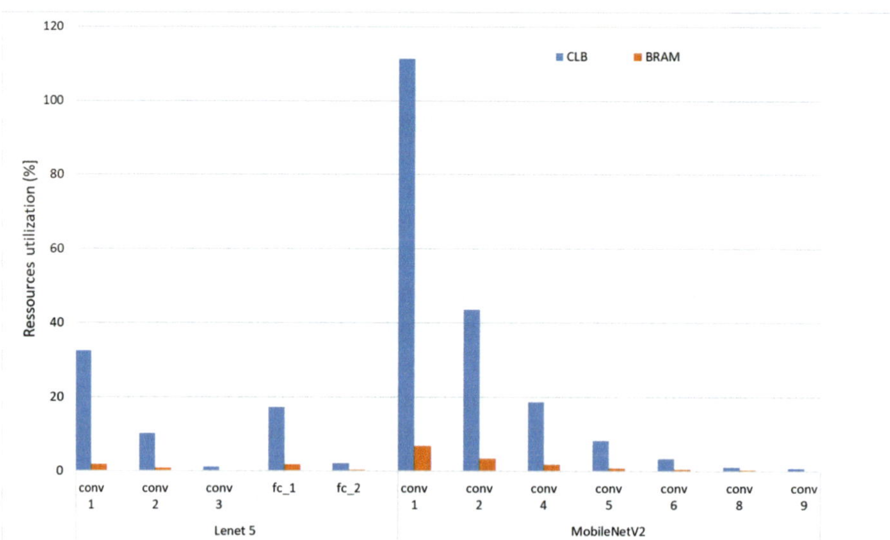

Figure 3.3 Synthesis results of different configurations of the proposed architecture

Figure 3.3 shows the percentages of FPGA resource utilization when executing the different layers of Lenet5 and MobilenetV2 given in Table 3.1. The processing of each type of layer requires a particular configuration of the proposed architecture. A configuration of the proposed architecture depends on the number of filter rows, ifmap rows, and ofmap rows. We observe a correlation between the variation in the size of the proposed architecture and the consumption of the CLBs. The larger the configuration, the greater the resource consumption. The consumption of the BRAM memory blocks depends on the size of the input image or the ifmaps. This means that the memory size remains fixed for a fixed input image/feature-map size, and the size of the filter. Particularly, for the conv_1 of MobileNetV2, we notice that the number of CLBs exceeds the maximum number of CLBs available in the FPGA targeted in these experiments. This representation shows that the proposed architecture remains flexible to support all convolution layer sizes. We just need to aim for a prototyping platform that provides the necessary logic resources for mapping all layers.

3.6.2.2 Latency

Figure 3.4 shows the latency performance of the proposed architecture for each convolution type. It can be observed that the proposed architecture is up to 71.2× (conv_1, Lenet5) faster w.r.t. single RISC-V CPU [2]. The total execution time for each convolution type for the proposed architecture is divided into ifmap loading time, filter loading time, data reuse, and overlap between communication-computation including time required for the PSum to traverse across their respective columns to store the computed ofmap. The breakdown of latency reports that data reuse and overlap between communication and computation significantly improve the overall execution time in the proposed architecture. For latency comparison of the proposed architecture with RISC-V CPU, the time required for access L2 to load data into IGBs is also considered for a fair comparison.

The overall speedup of MobileNetV2 convolution layers is up to 2.07× w.r.t. Eyeriss v2 [16, 17]. Here, Eyeriss v2 executes all layers of MobileNetV2 while the proposed architecture executes convolution layers (Table 3.1). These results are obtained through RTL simulations.

3.6.2.3 Energy consumption

Different hardware modules of the proposed architecture involved in different execution phases for each convolution type are shown in Table 3.3. The explanation of each phase is as follows: (1) Phase A represents data loading from all IGBs, (2) Phase B represents data reuse, (3) Phase C represents data loading from row IGBs, and (4) Phase D represents computation in NPE array. The results in this section are obtained through hardware emulation.

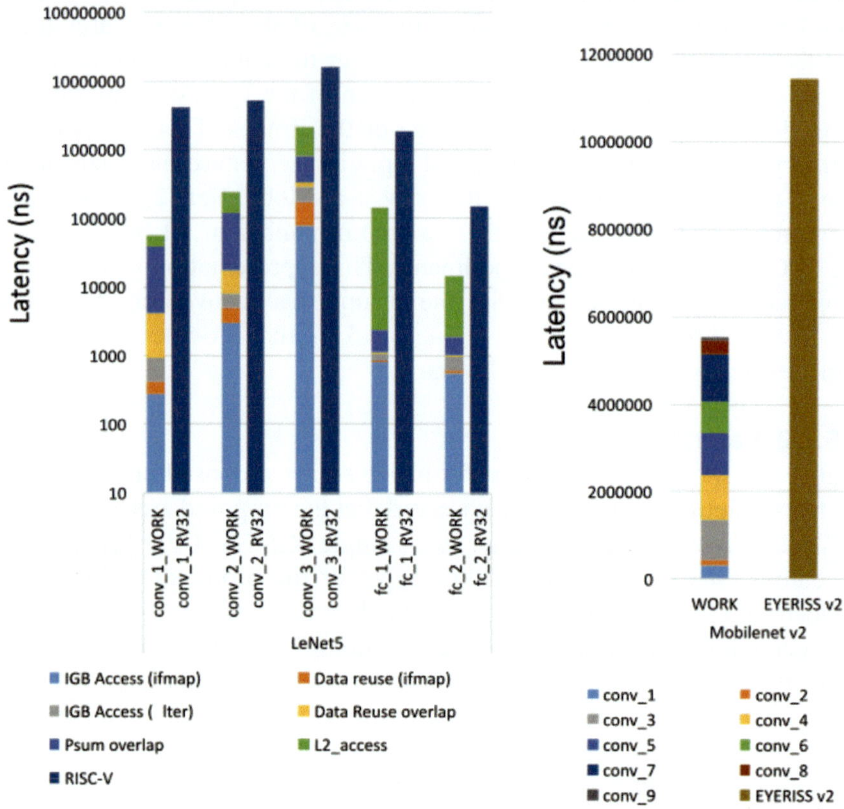

Figure 3.4 Breakdown of latency (ns). For the proposed architecture, the convolution layer includes memory accesses and computations. WORK = This Work, RV32 = RISC-V CPU.

Table 3.3 Different execution phases in the proposed architecture

Execution Phase	NPE array	AINoC	IGB row	IGB column	OGB	NGC
A	X	X	X	X		X
B	X	X				X
C	X	X	X			X
D	X	X			X	X

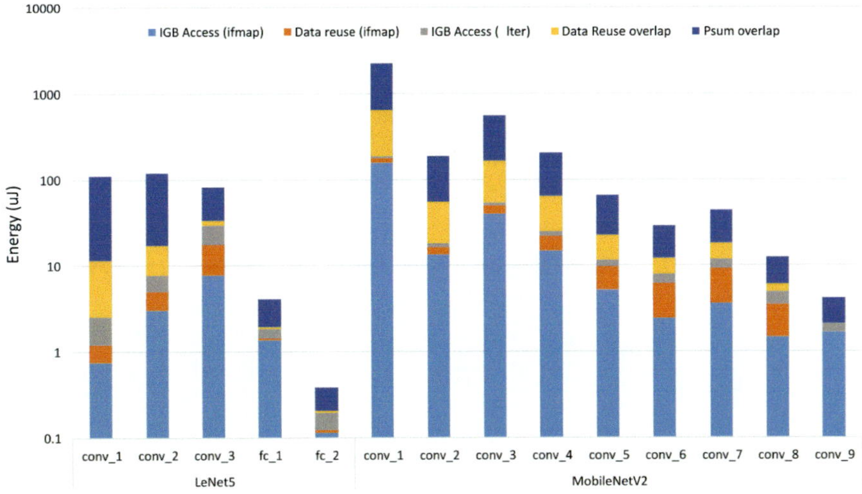

Figure 3.5 Energy consumption (uJ) of the proposed architecture

Using Table 3.3, energy consumption for each execution phase for the proposed architecture is computed. Figure 3.5 shows the total energy consumption of the proposed architecture per convolution layer. It can be observed that a significant energy saving is achieved because following input data loading into the NPEs, which have direct connections with IGBs, the proposed architecture applies data reuse by sending the loaded input data to target NPEs in the array. Notably, a significant energy saving can be observed during the loading of ifmap data because IGBs are not accessed during this phase (Phase B). Due to different design flows i.e., Eyeriss v2 is ASIC and the proposed architecture is FPGA, it is not a fair comparison between the two architectures, and also due to the unavailability of design flow scripts for RISCV CPU [2], we concluded to exclude the energy consumption comparisons for both architectures with the proposed architecture.

3.6.2.4 Energy efficiency

The proposed architecture can reach up to 2498 MOPS/W on an FPGA target for fc_1 of LeNet5 because of a single row with a large number of columns configuration, i.e., 1×84 (Figure 3.6). However, conv_2 of LeNet5 and conv_9 of MobileNetV2 have the lowest energy efficiency because in these layers there is less scope for optimized computation due to a low ratio

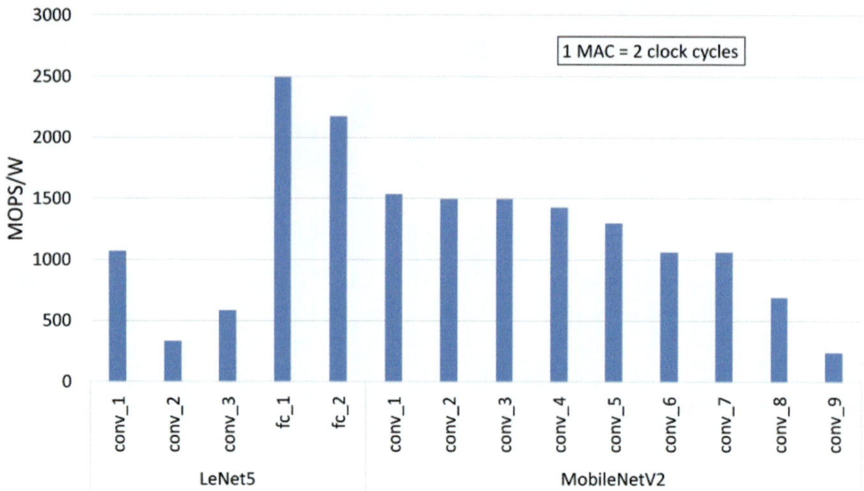

Figure 3.6 Energy efficiency (MOPS/W) of the proposed architecture

between ifmaps size and filter size (conv_2, LeNet5) or single row with few number of columns (conv_9, MobileNetV2).

3.7 Conclusion

This work presented a new flexible and scalable interconnect-based dataflow architecture, which can leverage data reuse and overlap between communication and computation to accelerate CNNs. We evaluated the proposed architecture results using LeNet5 and MobileNetV2 to show its adaptability to different types of DNNs. We then compared the latency results with state-of-the-art architectures. The proposed architecture is implemented (place and route) onto the Versal ACAP VCK190 kit featuring XCVC19022VSVA2197 FPGA partition. The experimental results show that the proposed architecture can speedup LeNet5 convolution layers by up to 71.2× in latency performance w.r.t. a RISC-V-based CPU and also speedup MobileNetV2 convolution layers by up to 2.07× in latency performance w.r.t. Eyeriss v2. We plan, in the future, to continue implementing optimisation techniques in the proposed architecture to better its energy efficiency and make the most of the underlying AINoC for accelerating complete Convolution Neural Networks execution.

Acknowledgements

This work was conducted within the scope of the European NEUROKIT2E project, funded by the European Union's Horizon Europe research and innovation program, under grant agreement number 101112268.

References

[1] A. Parashar et al., "SCNN: An Accelerator for Compressed-Sparse Convolutional Neural Networks," in arXiv. 2017 https://doi.org/10.48550/ARXIV.1708.04485

[2] A. Pullini et al., "Mr. Wolf: An Energy-Precision Scalable Parallel Ultra Low Power SoC for IoT Edge Processing," in IEEE JSSC, 2019, vol. 54, 7, pp. 1970–1981. https://doi.org/10.1109/JSSC.2019.2912307

[3] C. Farabet et al., "NeuFlow: A runtime reconfigurable dataflow processor for vision," in CVPR WORKSHOPS. IEEE, USA, 2011, pp. 109–116. https://doi.org/10.1109/CVPRW.2011.5981829

[4] D. Bhatt et al., "CNN Variants for Computer Vision: History, Architecture, Application, Challenges, and Future Scope," in Electronics: Ambient Assistive Methodologies/Frameworks for Internet of Medical Things, 2021, vol. 10, https://doi.org/10.3390/electronics10202470

[5] E. S. Shin et al., ń Round-robin Arbiter Design and Generation," in Proceedings of the 15th ISSS. Japan, 2002, pp. 243–248. https://doi.org/10.1145/581199.581253

[6] G. Sapijaszko et al., "An Overview of Recent Convolutional Neural Network Algorithms for Image Recognition," in 61st MWSCAS. 2018. Canada. https://doi.org/10.1109/MWSCAS.2018.8623911

[7] H. Kwon et al., "MAERI: Enabling Flexible Dataflow Mapping over DNN Accelerators via Reconfigurable Interconnects," in ACM SIGPLAN Notices. Vol. 53. 2018. pp. 461–475. https://doi.org/10.1145/3296957.3173176

[8] H. Krichene et al., "Analysis of on-chip communication properties in accelerator architectures for Deep Neural Networks," in 15th IEEE/ACM NOCS. USA, 2021. pp. 9–14. https://doi.org/10.1145/3479876.3481588

[9] H. Krichene et al., "AINoC: New Interconnect for Future Deep Neural Network Accelerators," in DASIP, 2023. pp 55–69.

[10] K. Sankaralingam et al., "Distributed Micro-architectural Protocols in the TRIPS Prototype Processor," in 39th MICRO'06. USA. 2006. https://doi.org/10.1109/MICRO.2006.19

collaborate to train ML algorithms under the coordination of a central server, without sharing their private datasets with other parties [10].

To train a federated model a central server distributes to the participating clients an initial model and the training parameters. Then the following steps take place:

1. each participant trains the received model using their private dataset, producing a local model and then sends it to the server;
2. the server aggregates all local models into a global one;
3. the global model is distributed to all clients.

Figure 4.2 illustrates this process which can be repeated for multiple learning steps and stopped when a designated criterion is met.

FL is considered in two different configurations, in general [10]:

- Cross-device: clients are computing systems with limited computing capabilities, varying device availability and small datasets, e.g. IoT devices or smartphones.
- Cross-silo: clients are computing systems with high computational power, high reliability and large datasets (data silos), such as centralized and enterprise systems (typically 2-100).

In traditional centralized machine learning environments, a device or an organization must train a model on its own self-collected data. In practice, these devices or organizations may not have access to sufficiently large data sets and the computing capabilities necessary to train an effective model. Additionally, data privacy concerns and intellectual property rights limit collaboration between parties. FL addresses these challenges by enabling collaboration between multiple parties to jointly train effective ML models with large, diverse datasets collected from all members of the federation [11]. As the produced models are the only information shared among federation members, local data never leave the participating devices enabling data owners to keep their data private. Importantly, FL scales well because additional members can contribute to model training without any burden to other members and with reduced data traffic among them.

FL is employed in several operations of cybersecurity such as attack detection, anomaly detection, trust management, authentication and other IoT related tasks [12, 13, 14, 15]. FL is also effective in malicious URL and Denial-of-Service (DoS) attacks detection [16, 17].

In malware detection, research in FL employment is mainly focused on cross-device FL where federation members (clients) are smartphones [18, 19] or IoT devices [20], while limited effort has been spent on malware detection

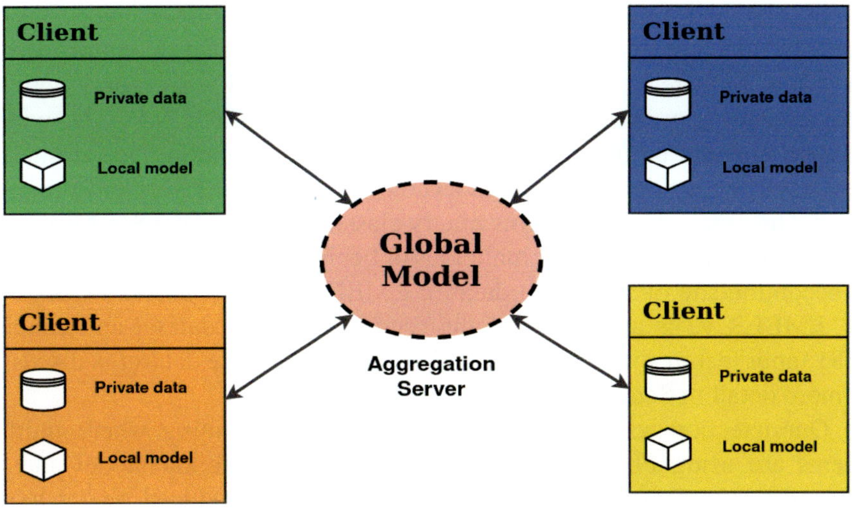

Figure 4.2 Federated Learning configuration.

using cross-silo FL configurations. In our work, we propose a cross-silo FL-based malware detection method, where federation members are different Edge or near-Edge devices deployed to provide security to different organizational networks. The devices collect large amounts of data and have higher computational capabilities relatively to the devices considered in cross-device configurations.

State-of-the-art malware detection approaches employ neural networks architectures to train models for sample classification as either malicious or benign [8, 9]. In our system, we employ a similar neural network [21] that can effectively learn to detect malware from the training data, while being able to fit in Edge or near-Edge devices. Some preliminary results of this work were presented in [26].

4.3 Architecture

Our proposed architecture consists of a FL cross-silo configuration as shown in Figure 4.3. Multiple participating members, indicated as clients, collaboratively train a global malware detection model, and a server is responsible for all communications as well as the aggregation of the global model. Each client owns and trains with some large amount of local private data which it does not share with the other clients nor the server.

In training, each client uses the same feed forward neural network, i.e. the same architecture and training parameters, an increasingly popular method for malware detection [8, 9]. Specifically, we employ a neural network deployed in [21]. We adopt its architecture because it is versatile, widely adopted and can be fitted in devices with limited computing power such as near-edge or edge devices. The model consists of 3 linear layers and a dropout layer. The output layer performs binary classification using a SoftMax layer, classifying a sample as either malicious or benign. We adapt the model in [21] to accommodate our different dataset: EMBER v2 [22] instead of EMBER v1. EMBER v2 is an update on the original EMBER dataset and contains 2381 input features instead of the 2351 used in [21]. The dataset is discussed in more detail in Section 1.4.1.

Our detection system, operates in two modes: (a) training, where multiple clients are using FL to collaboratively train the detection model and (b) detection, where each participating client uses the produced global model to detect malware.

In training mode, the FL-based training process takes place in multiple steps. In each step the following process occurs: (i) each client trains a local model using its own private data, (ii) each client sends the produced local model to the server, (iii) the server aggregates all local models, producing a global model and (iv) the server distributes the global model to all clients. Then, the clients can use the global model to measure the model's performance against their private datasets. The process can be repeated for multiple steps to improve the model's performance further, until a satisfactory model is achieved, considering the time and processing constraints of the clients or until no further accuracy improvement is achieved.

After training is complete, in detection mode, all participating clients have received a copy of the final global model from the server. Each client can use this model to detect malware in their own systems and networks, independently from all other clients. Finally, the clients can return to training mode to refresh and retrain their model with new data.

4.4 Experiments

We evaluate the performance of cross-silo FL measuring the malware detection accuracy on a benchmark dataset containing features from malware and benign files. To further explore the effectiveness of FL, we consider multiple FL training setups measuring how the detection rate is affected by the number of learning steps, the number of participating clients and the commonality in the participating clients' datasets. Furthermore, to demonstrate the benefits of FL for the participants, we also train a centralized model of the same architecture and parameters and evaluate its performance different training dataset sizes. To conduct the experiments, we employ flower [23], a popular FL framework, for training the federated models, in conjunction with Pytorch [24].

4.4.1 Dataset

In all our experiments we use the EMBER v2 dataset [22], a publicly available benchmark dataset, which contains features extracted from both malware and benign samples using static analysis. We use EMBER because there are no widely available standard datasets; this is a well-known problem in cybersecurity research. Although it does not distribute the sample binary files, due to privacy concerns, EMBER is common choice in malware detection and analysis because of three factors: (i) its sufficient size, (ii) its set of features and (iii) it contains features of malware and benign samples.

EMBER v2 contains 2381 features per sample, extracted using static analysis from 1.1 million Windows Portable Executables (PE). More specifically for training, the dataset contains 600.000 samples labelled as either benign or malicious (300.000 benign and 300.000 malicious), and 300.000 unlabelled samples. The dataset also contains 200.000 samples labelled as either benign or malicious (100.000 benign and 100.000 malicious) to be used as a dedicated benchmark testing set. In our experiments we only use labelled samples, 600.000 for training the neural networks and 200.000 for testing the produced models.

4.4.2 Evaluation results

In the first experiment we consider a FL setup where 2 participating clients train a common model for 10 learning steps using the entire dataset. Thus, each client trains each local model with 300.000 data samples. We measure the accuracy, precision. recall and f1 score of the model on the test set for each step. Table 4.1 summarizes the results of the experiment. For comparison we also train a centralized model on the full dataset, 600.000 data samples and we measure an accuracy of 0,9338 on the test set.

Figure 4.3 plots the accuracy of the FL model for multiple learning steps. The orange line denotes the accuracy of the centralized model as reference trained with the entire EMBER dataset of 600K samples. The results show that the accuracy of FL increases with the increasing number of training loops

Next, we consider a case where different organizations or different devices in the same organization that participate in a FL setup, have common data samples in their private data. As attackers and malware authors use the same malware samples to infect multiple targets and as organizations process a large amount of malware on daily basis it seems a likely scenario that participants will have some degree of commonality in their private datasets. Thus, we evaluate whether the presence of overlapping samples in the participants' training sets influences the accuracy of the produced FL model. We consider different dataset overlap percentages between the participants for 2 and 10 participating clients. Tables 4.3 and 4.4 present the results of the experiments for 2 and 10 participants respectively for 2 FL training steps.

Table 4.3 Accuracy on test set of FL models for different dataset overlaps for 2 clients.

	2 Clients			
Overlap percentage	**Accuracy**	**Precision**	**Recall**	**F1 Score**
0	0,9111	0,9012	0,9236	0,9123
5	0,9166	0,9139	0,92	0,9169
10	0,9045	0,9039	0,9054	0,9046
15	0,9129	0,9057	0,9218	0,9137
20	0,9114	0,902	0,9231	0,9124
25	0,918	0,9117	0,9256	0,9186
30	0,9125	0,9063	0,9201	0,9131
35	0,9124	0,9098	0,9157	0,9128
40	0,9173	0,9127	0,9228	0,9178
45	0,9319	0,9267	0,9378	0,9322
50	0,9262	0,9197	0,934	0,9268

Table 4.4 Accuracy on test set of FL models for different dataset overlaps for 10 clients.

	10 Clients			
Overlap percentage	**Accuracy**	**Precision**	**Recall**	**F1 Score**
0	0,9144	0,9091	0,921	0,915
5	0,9162	0,9108	0,9229	0,9168
10	0,9154	0,9086	0,9238	0,9161
15	0,9167	0,9096	0,9255	0,9175
20	0,9171	0,9121	0,9233	0,9176
25	0,9169	0,909	0,9267	0,9177
30	0,9171	0,9114	0,9242	0,9177
35	0,9178	0,9138	0,9227	0,9182
40	0,9146	0,9059	0,9254	0,9155
45	0,9179	0,9093	0,9285	0,9188
50	0,9174	0,9114	0,9247	0,918

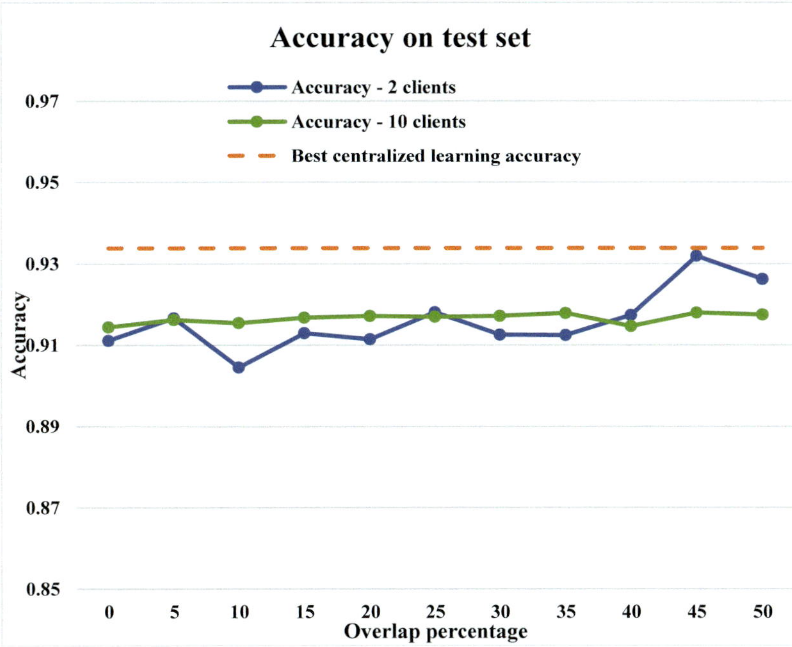

Figure 4.5 Federated model accuracy for different dataset overlaps.

Figure 4.5 plots the accuracy on the test set of the FL models produced as a function of the overlap (common subset) of the clients' training data, i.e. x=5 indicates 5% common data in the client datasets. The blue and green lines depict the accuracy of the models trained by 2 and 10 clients respectively. The orange line denotes the accuracy of the centralized model as reference trained with the entire EMBER dataset of 600K samples. As we observe in both setups, accuracy seems to be effectively independent of the common samples present in the participants' private data even in the extreme case of a 50% overlap, meaning that the produced models do not overfit on the common data.

Finally, to showcase the benefits of FL for organizations, we consider a scenario where a single organization or device is not participating in a FL setup but instead trains its own centralized model using its own private data. We consider organizations of different sizes that have different training data availability. We train a centralized model (no federation present) of the same architecture and parameters as in the previous FL setups with different dataset sizes. Table 4.5 summarizes the results.

Table 4.5 Accuracy on test set of centralized models for different dataset sizes.

Number of samples	Accuracy	Precision	Recall	F1 Score
5000	0,8443	0,8299	0,8662	0,8477
10000	0,8482	0,8428	0,8828	0,8623
50000	0,8949	0,8791	0,9156	0,897
100000	0,9126	0,904	0,9232	0,9135
600000	0,9338	0,9271	0,9417	0,9343

Figure 4.6 plots the accuracy for the centralized (non-federated) system as a function of the dataset size. The blue line denotes the best FL accuracy we measured in our experiments for reference. The results indicate that a data set size of 600K is necessary in the centralized (non-federated) case for achieving high accuracy that reaches above 93% and matches the accuracy of the FL system. This result is the reference accuracy towards which we evaluate the performance of the federated system cases. Importantly, when considering Figure 4.3 as well, the plot demonstrates the benefit of FL for small organizations and near-edge devices with limited data availability that do not have access to large datasets to train centralized models. We also note that even that even organizations and devices that

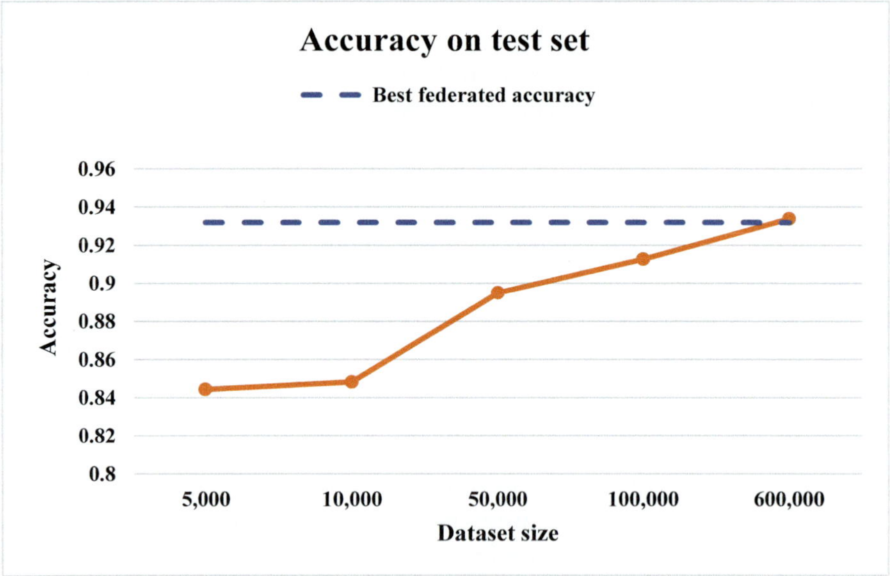

Figure 4.6 Centralized learning model's performance for different dataset sizes.

have access to large datasets can benefit from FL, as a model generated with contributions from multiple participants is trained on a potentially more diverse dataset with malware and benign samples coming from different networks.

4.5 Conclusions

Federated learning constitutes an effective and efficient machine learning technology of classification in malware detection. It provides significant advantages over centralized machine learning solutions, because it enables distributed building of effective malware detection models without source data exchange among members of a federation. We demonstrate that with the adoption of NNs for model training, members of a federation achieve high malware detection accuracy, exceeding, in cases, the accuracy achieved with centralized machine learning methods. Importantly, all members of the federation achieve this accuracy, which would be unattainable if they were limited to training using only their own local data. This advantage also provides a motivation for organizations to participate in federations. In addition to the performance and privacy advantages, federated learning scales well to large federations, due to the low data exchange, and accommodates systems and devices with limited processing power, because the employed NNs of the clients can be efficiently executed even in low-power computational environments. In our work, we considered a centralized aggregating server and Edge or near-Edge devices that provide security in their respective local networks as the federation participants. When considering real word deployments of such setups, additional design parameters should be taken into account. Firstly, the Edge devices should have the computational power and memory to fit and train the chosen NN. In our implementation we specifically used a small model that solves the malware detection task adequately, while requiring low computational power and small memory footprint. Additionally, as discussed in Section 1.3, during training all devices should be available for training and a reliable network connection should be present between each participant and the server. After the training is complete, during inference, no such limitations are present. Finally, the power consumption, latency costs and network communications overhead should be explored; we leave that as future work.

Acknowledgements

Part of D. Serpanos' research was conducted at the Industrial Systems Institute/ATHENA under funding and support by the Hellenic Foundation for Research and Innovation (H.F.R.I.) under the "2nd Call for H.F.R.I. Research Projects to support Faculty Members & Researchers" (Project Number: 4012).

References

[1] D. Serpanos, P. Michalopoulos, G. Xenos, and V. Ieronymakis, "Sisyfos: A Modular and Extendable Open Malware Analysis Platform." Applied Sciences, 11(7), p. 2980, 3/2021, https://doi.org/10.3390/app11072980.

[2] A. Shalaginov, S. Banin, A. Dehghantanha, and K. Franke, "Machine Learning Aided Static Malware Analysis: A Survey and Tutorial." In A. Dehghantanha, M. Conti, and T. Dargahi (Eds) Eds., Cyber Threat Intelligence. Advances in Information Security, vol. 70. Cham: Springer International Publishing, 2018, pp. 7–45.

[3] A. Moser, C. Kruegel, and E. Kirda, "Limits of Static Analysis for Malware Detection." In Proceedings of 23rd Annual Computer Security Applications Conference (ACSAC 2007), Miami Beach, FL, USA, 10–14 December 2007, pp. 421–430.

[4] A. Mohaisen, O. Alrawi, and M. Mohaisen, "AMAL: High-fidelity, behavior-based automated malware analysis and classification." Computers & Security, vol. 52, pp. 251–266, Jul. 2015.

[5] W. Li, J. Ge, and G. Dai, "Detecting Malware for Android Platform: An SVM-Based Approach." In Proceedings of 2nd International Conference on Cyber Security and Cloud Computing, New York, NY, USA: IEEE, Nov. 2015, pp. 464–469.

[6] F.C.C. Garcia and F.P. Muga II, "Random Forest for Malware Classification." arXiv, Sep. 25, 2016. [Online]. Available: http://arxiv.org/abs/1609.07770.

[7] R. Vinayakumar, et al. "Robust Intelligent Malware Detection Using Deep Learning." IEEE Access, vol. 7, pp. 46717–46738, 2019.

[8] E. Raff, et al, "Classifying Sequences of Extreme Length with Constant Memory Applied to Malware Detection." AAAI, 35(11), pp. 9386–9394, May 2021, https://doi.org/10.1609/aaai.v35i11.17131.

[9] L. Li, Y. Fan, M. Tse, and K.-Y. Lin, "A review of applications in federated learning." In Computers & Industrial Engineering, vol. 149, p. 106854, Nov. 2020, https://doi.org/10.1016/j.cie.2020.106854.

[10] P. Kairouz et al., "Advances and Open Problems in Federated Learning," MAL, vol. 14, no. 1–2, pp. 1–210, Jun. 2021, https://doi.org/10.1561/2200000083.

[11] T. Zhang, et al, "Federated Learning for the Internet of Things: Applications, Challenges, and Opportunities." In IEEE Internet of Things, 5(1), pp. 24–29, Mar. 2022, https://doi.org/10.1109/IOTM.004.2100182.

[12] M. Alazab, et al., "Federated Learning for Cybersecurity: Concepts, Challenges, and Future Directions," IEEE Trans. Ind. Inf., 18(5), pp. 3501–3509, May 2022, https://doi.org/10.1109/TII.2021.3119038.

[13] M. Venkatasubramanian, A. H. Lashkari, and S. Hakak, "IoT Malware Analysis Using Federated Learning: A Comprehensive Survey." In IEEE Access, vol. 11, pp. 5004–5018, 2023.

[14] T. D. Nguyen, et al, "DÏoT: A Federated Self-learning Anomaly Detection System for IoT." In Proceedings IEEE 39th International Conference on Distributed Computing Systems (ICDCS), Dallas, TX, USA: IEEE, Jul. 2019, pp. 756–767. https://doi.org/10.1109/ICDCS.2019.00080.

[15] V. Mothukuri, et al, "Federated-Learning-Based Anomaly Detection for IoT Security Attacks." IEEE Internet of Things, 9(4), pp. 2545–2554, Feb. 2022, https://doi.org/10.1109/JIOT.2021.3077803.

[16] E. Khramtsova, C. Hammerschmidt, S. Lagraa, and R. State, "Federated Learning For Cyber Security: SOC Collaboration For Malicious URL Detection." In Proceedings IEEE 40th International Conference on Distributed Computing Systems (ICDCS), Singapore, Nov. 2020, pp. 1316–1321. https://doi.org/10.1109/ICDCS47774.2020.00171.

[17] R. Doriguzzi-Corin and D. Siracusa, "FLAD: Adaptive Federated Learning for DDoS Attack Detection." arXiv, Aug. 23, 2022. [Online]. Available: http://arxiv.org/abs/2205.06661.

[18] R. Gálvez, V. Moonsamy, and C. Diaz, "Less is More: A privacy-respecting Android malware classifier using federated learning." In Proceedings on Privacy Enhancing Technologies, 2021(4), pp. 96–116, Oct. 2021, https://doi.org/10.2478/popets-2021-0062

[19] R.-H. Hsu et al., "A Privacy-Preserving Federated Learning System for Android Malware Detection Based on Edge Computing." In Proceedings 15th Asia Joint Conference on Information Security (AsiaJCIS), Taipei, Taiwan, Aug. 2020, pp. 128–136.

[20] V. Rey, P. M. S. Sánchez, A. H. Celdrán, G. Bovet, and M. Jaggi, "Federated Learning for Malware Detection in IoT Devices," Computer Networks, vol. 204, p. 108693, Feb. 2022, https://doi.org/10.1016/j.comnet.2021.108693.

[21] S. Pramanik and H. Teja, "EMBER - Analysis of Malware Dataset Using Convolutional Neural Networks." In Proceedings 2019 Third International Conference on Inventive Systems and Control (ICISC), Coimbatore, India, Jan. 2019, pp. 286–291, https://doi.org/10.1109/ICISC44355.2019.9036424.

[22] H. S. Anderson and P. Roth, "EMBER: An Open Dataset for Training Static PE Malware Machine Learning Models." arXiv, Apr. 16, 2018, https://doi.org/10.48550/arXiv.1804.04637.

[23] D. J. Beutel et al., "Flower: A Friendly Federated Learning Research Framework." arXiv, Mar. 5, 2022, https://doi.org/10.48550/arXiv.2007.14390.

[24] A. Paszke et al., "PyTorch: An Imperative Style, High-Performance Deep Learning Library." arXiv, Dec. 03, 2019, https://doi.org/10.48550/arXiv.1912.01703.

[25] "VirusTotal." https://www.virustotal.com/gui/.

[26] D. Serpanos and G. Xenos, "Federated Learning in Malware Detection," 2023 IEEE 28th International Conference on Emerging Technologies and Factory Automation (ETFA), Sinaia, Romania, 2023, pp. 1-4, https://doi.org/10.1109/ETFA54631.2023.10275578.

5

Image Signal Processor (ISP) Tuning using Machine Learning (ML) methods

Sepehr Bijani

NXP Semiconductors, Germany

Abstract

Image Signal Processor (ISP) is responsible for improving camera signal quality and producing high-quality images. ISP has a vast number of parameters which should be tunned based on both camera sensor and operating environment. Sensor related ISP parameters are tunned offline for each camera sensor. Parameters related to environment such as white balancing gains must be fine-tuned during the runtime. The offline phase is cumbersome and costly. At the same time, the runtime for fine-tuning should be fast and accurate. Therefore, the proposed tuning framework needs to achieve two goals at the same time: a) tune the sensor related parameters automatically in lab and b) fine-tuning ISP in the field with a runtime.

For the static parameters, a tuner finds the optimal parameters in lab condition. Tuning dynamic parameters needs a dataset with various scenes and corresponding optimal parameters. A data generation pipeline produces the dataset by running the tuner in a loop. An ML model is trained based on generated dataset as runtime for fine-tuning ISP.

Keywords: image signal processor, ISP, machine learning, ML, tuning, camera tuning.

DOI: 10.1201/9788743808633-5

5.1 Introduction and Background

5.1.1 Tuning problem

Improving System performance by changing bounded parameters respect to predefined Key Performance Indicator (KPI).

5.1.2 Image Signal processor (ISP)

ISP is a hardware or software component responsible for converting camera signal (Bayer Pattern Image) to perceivable image for human eye. It improves image quality by attenuating image artifacts. For achieving optimal performance in different environmental scenarios and various cameras, ISP has many parameters which should be tuned and optimized for different use cases. The tuning process is manual and costly. The effect of varying ISP parameters has a considerable impact on deep learning-based object detection systems, so having an automatic process and measuring the ISP performance will improve overall Advanced Driver Assistance Systems (ADAS) response [1].

Figure 5.1 Image Generation using ISP and Camera.

5.1.3 Mathematical Optimization Problem

Having a mathematical model for a system, the behavior of the system can be improved by defining an optimization problem as [2]:

$$\begin{aligned} \underset{x}{\text{minimize}} \quad & f(x) \\ \text{subject to} \quad & g_i(x) \leq 0, \quad i = 1, \ldots, m \\ & h_j(x) = 0, \quad j = 1, \ldots, p \end{aligned}$$

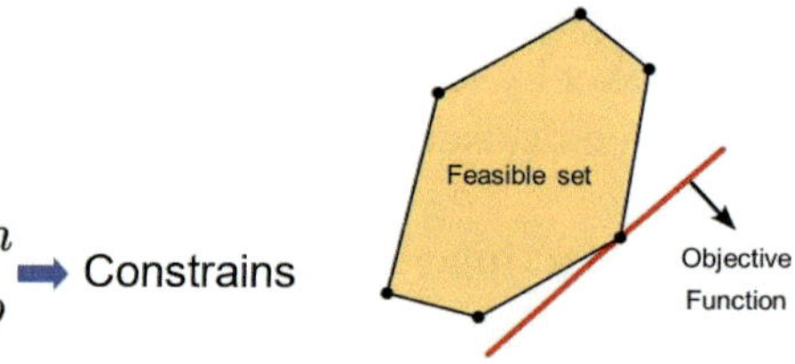

Figure 5.2 Linear Optimization Problem [3].

Where cost function f(x) models the KPI needed to improve system performance. In a tuning problem, f(x) is blocking, and high number of f(x) calls will be impractically slow. As a result, running f with a parameter set x is time consuming, and any solver for tuning problem should find optimal parameters with the smallest number of iterations. An example of optimization problem is Linear Programming (LP) where f, g, and h are linear function and define a polyhedron. Changing parameter x will move a linear function across the feasibility set as show in Figure 5.2.

5.1.4 Static and Dynamic Parameters in ISP

Different algorithms utilized in ISP which have individual parameters. Each algorithm tries to attenuate artifacts from a specific source:

a) Static Parameters: Algorithms responsible for improving artifacts originated from camera sensor have static parameters which should be tuned only once.
b) Dynamic Parameters: Algorithm responsible for improving artifacts due to light condition and environmental phenomena have dynamic parameters which should be updated during runtime.

The static parameters which are related to camera sensor characteristics can be tuned once for the specific camera. After tuning the ISP for the specific camera, the parameters can be fixed in configuration file for deployment.

Tuning dynamic parameters improves the image quality in different environmental conditions. The dynamic parameters should be updated during runtime to guaranty best image quality performance.

5.1.5 State of Art

The tuning process is done manually by experts. Each ISP algorithm is responsible for reducing specific artifact in image and the expert can measure the artifact intensity using a specific KPI. Then by changing the ISP parameters and try and error, the expert can find best parameters combination for specific camera sensor.

For tuning dynamic parameters, expert do the same process, but for a range of environmental conditions. That means, first a set of input ISP images (Bayer Pattern) are captured from sensor in different environmental condition, then expert should tune the ISP for each one of the input images. ISP has an algorithm for gathering the statistical data for Bayer pattern image. Having the statical data for all images and corresponding optimal ISP parameters, one can make a "decision tree" which changes the parameters on flight based on statistical data provided by ISP.

5.2 Automatic ISP Tuning

The automatic tuning process should be done for both Dynamic and Static parameters.

5.2.1 KPIs for Artifact Attenuation

For measuring ISP performance, various KPIs should be defined. Each KPI measures the intensity of a specific artifact in image. It should be noted that there is no one to one relation between artifacts and ISP algorithms. In many cases one KPI could be used for tuning multiple ISP algorithms. The list of KPIs is [4]:

Table 5.1 KPIs for Measuring Image Artifacts.

Artifact	ISP block	KPI
Noise	Noise Reduction Block(s)	PSNR
Loss of detail	Sharpness Correction	MTF50
Color Inaccuracy	Color Correction Matrix (CCM)	ΔE
Color Casting	White Balancing	ΔE

5.2.2 Static Parameters

The setup is done once in lab and a camera is attached to the capturing device. The captured Bayer pattern is fed to the ISP as input. The ISP generates an image. For measuring the performance of specific ISP algorithm in attenuating an artifact, corresponding KPI in Table 1 is used. ISP tuner can track KPI value for judging performance result of a set of parameters. ISP tuner changes the ISP parameters in multiple iterations and tries to optimize parameters based on KPI value. The process is iterative, and the iterative process is needed to be done only once for static ISP parameters as shown in Figure 5.3. The optimal value found by Tuner will be stored as fixed configuration for runtime.

Figure 5.3 Tuning ISP Static Parameters.

5.2.3 Dynamic Parameters and Runtime

Achieving optimal performance with dynamic parameters is harder. The parameters should be re-tuned to adapt environmental effects such as light condition, temperature, etc.

There are limitations in using same iterative approach for tuning static parameters:

1. The iterative approach makes it impossible to have optimal parameters per frame or even per minute.
2. Measuring the KPI during runtime is challenging since there is no reference for the scene captured by camera.

A proposal solution is to use a machine learning model which can map image statistical data to optimal parameters. All ISPs measure image statistical data and provide it per frame. The dataset can be created by utilizing same tuning procedure mentioned for tuning statistical parameters in a loop as demonstrated in Figure 5.4.

E: All desired environmental conditions which ISP should operate in.
For e in E
{
1. Run tuner for optimizing ISP.
2. Store Optimal ISP parameters + ISP statistical data for the scene.
}

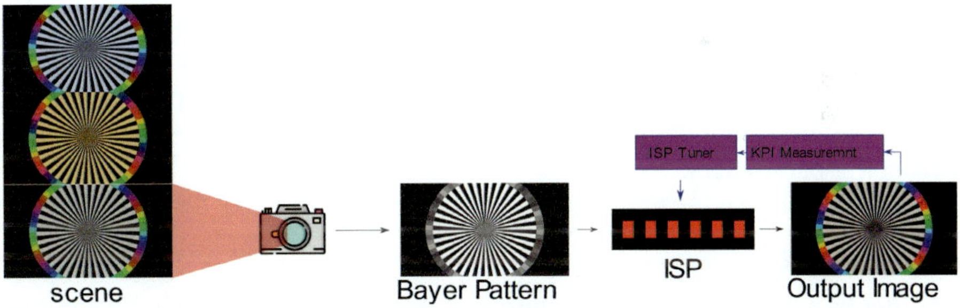

Figure 5.4 Dynamic Parameters Data Generation.

In theory, a Neural Network (NN) should be able to predict optimal values for dynamic parameters after training; however, an NN creates a high computation load during inference, so a more efficient solution is needed.

In this paper, a gradient boost model is proposed for inferencing the optimal parameters. Gradient boosting models are trainable decision trees. Unlike NN which use Directed acyclic graphs (DAGs) as underlaying data structure for training and inferencing, gradient boost (GB) utilizes trees which are simpler data structures [5]. GB models are fast to inference and has similar performance as NNs for tabular data which exactly matches the use case and dataset we have for dynamic tuning application.

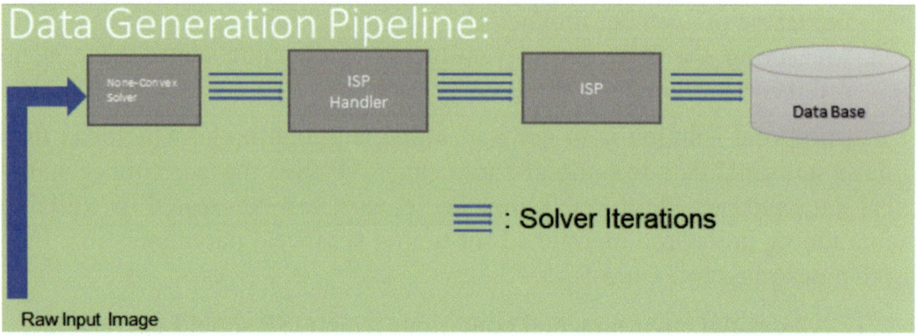

Figure 5.5 Storing Optimal Parameters and ISP Statistical Data for Training ML model.

5.2.4 Test Setup

Testing the proposed methods for tuning static and dynamic parameter are done with Solectrix SoftISP SXIVE[1]. The ISP runs on PC with dedicated graphic card. The tuner uses 16 cores CPU to speed up the process in lab for finding static parameters in ISP.

Same tuner is utilized to create a dataset of ISP statistical data and optimal parameters for ten lighting color temperature. The dataset is then used for training a GB model named XGboost as runtime. The trained model then runs on single core with minimum load on the same machine to update White Balancing parameters.

5.2.5 Results

The demo software (SW) is instantiated with init button. ISP with random parameters is run and the ISP output image is shown to the user. The user can select the boundaries of the Color Checker (CC) board inside the image then press "Tune". The SW will crop the image to find cc board and samples

[1] sxive.com

patches from the board and shows the sampling areas to the user (Annotated CC). Then, tuning process begins. In Figure 5.6 the process for finding a better optimum point is illustrated as tuner progress. The measured ΔE for all color blocks in color checkerboard is calculated and aggregated as Mean Squared Error (MSE) of ΔE values:

$$\mathrm{MSE}(\Delta\mathrm{E}) = \sum_{k=0}^{23} \frac{(\Delta\mathrm{E}_k)^2}{24}.$$

The SW results in Figure 5.6 can be interpreted as:

"ISP output" shows ISP output image for the current iteration, and "Best Config" shows the best result found by tuner until the current iteration. When tuner iterates over different configurations, it generates various "ISP outputs"

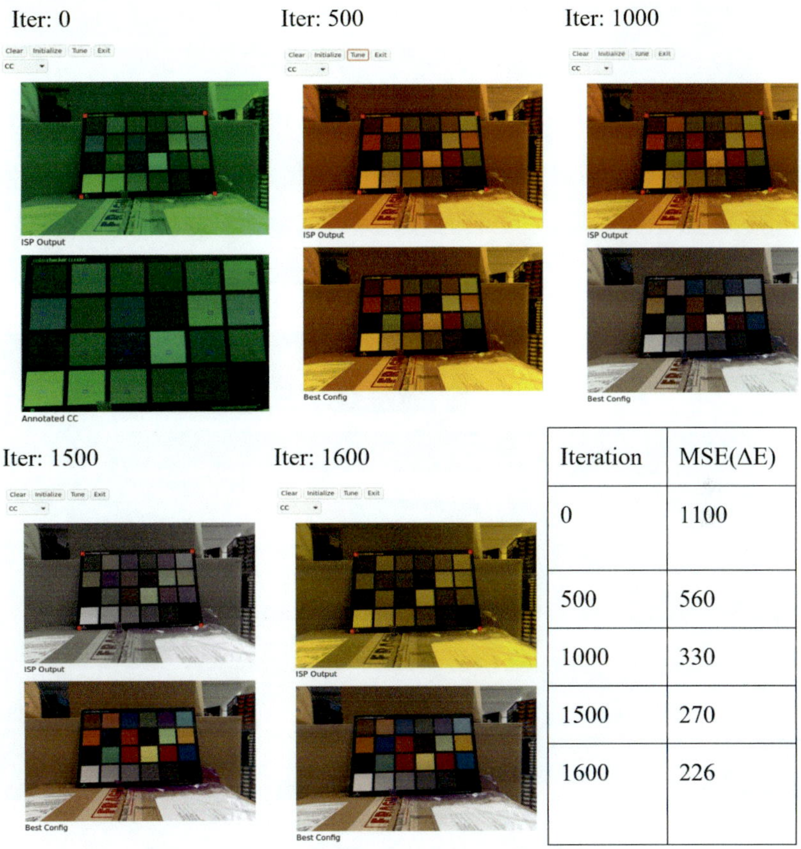

Iteration	MSE(ΔE)
0	1100
500	560
1000	330
1500	270
1600	226

Figure 5.6 Offline Tuning Results for Color Correction Matrix Tuning.

and corresponding KPI values; Based on observed KPI value, tuner guesses a better parameter set for the next iteration. As iterations go on, tuner can find better parameter sets which results in better KPI values, so as it can be seen, the "Best Config" image is improved when tuner progresses.

White balancing (WB) is the algorithm chosen for dynamic tuning. Same tuner finds optimal parameter for various light conditions and intensities in

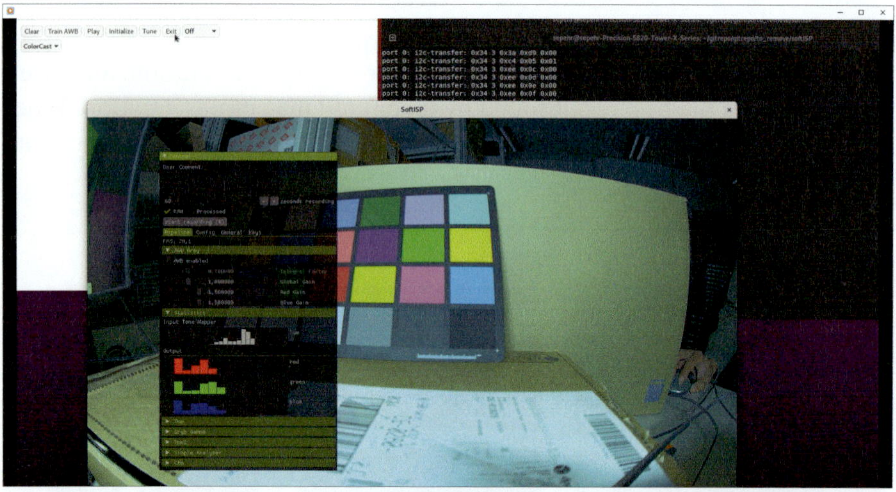

No WB

XGboost WB

Figure 5.7 Runtime Result of Trained XGboost WB.

lab in a loop as explained in Figure 5.4. The generated dataset maps image histogram to optimal WB configuration is used to train a XGboost model. The ISP has its own Automatic White Balancing (AWB), but we turned it off to show the effectiveness our of XGboost WB. The results are shown in Figure 5.7 without and with white balancing under blue light source.

5.3 Conclusion

Tuning ISP was conventionally a cumbersome, costly, and suboptimal task. The iterative process should have been done for combination of numerous ISPs and cameras. In pursue of a more automated solution, the proposed method tries to distinguish parameters based on static/dynamic nature. The parameters which are related to specific camera, can be tuned in lab, and the optimal parameters will be fixed as static parameters. For ISP algorithms which attenuates environmental impact on image quality, a runtime should fine-tune the ISP in the field. The runtime algorithm should be light enough to run on a restricted HW processor. For tuning both static and dynamic parameters, the paper presents a tuning framework to automate the process. A tuner finds optimal parameters for static parameters. A data generation pipeline utilizes same tuner in a loop for various environmental conditions. The generated data maps the statistical data provided by ISP to optimal parameters found by tuner. In the next steps, the trained GB model based on the generated dataset is used as a lightweighted runtime for tuning dynamic parameters in changing environmental condition.

References

[1] D. Molloy et al., "Impact of ISP Tuning on Object Detection," Journal of Imaging, vol. 9, no. 12, pp. 260-260, Nov. 2023, doi: https://doi.org/10.3390/jimaging9120260.

[2] S. Boyd and L. Vandenberghe, "Convex Optimization," Mar. 2004, doi: https://doi.org/10.1017/cbo9780511804441.

[3] https://en.wikipedia.org/wiki/Linear_programming.

[4] https://www.imatest.com/support/docs/23-2/colorcheck/

[5] T. Chen and C. Guestrin, "XGBoost: a Scalable Tree Boosting System," Proceedings of the 22nd ACM SIGKDD International Conference on Knowledge Discovery and Data Mining - KDD '16, pp. 785-794, 2016, doi: https://doi.org/10.1145/2939672.2939785.

6

Using Edge AI in IoT devices for Smart Agriculture: Autonomous Weeding

Christian Germain[1,2], Barna Keresztes[1,2], Aymeric Deshayes[1], and Jean-Pierre Da Costa[1,2]

[1]University of Bordeaux, CNRS, France
[2]Bordeaux Sciences Agro, France

Abstract

This paper presents the evolution of a vision system dedicated to automatic weeding, initially implemented on a NVIDIA Jetson Xavier board. This evolution aims to take advantage of a new computing board able to implement efficient artificial intelligence oriented computations, keeping a low power consumption, and a low cost, developed in the ANDANTE project. The paper presents the automatic weeding tool, the existing vision system and the weeding data used to train the system. It also describes the specifications of the new board and the adaptation needed in order to integrate the previous algorithm in this new board. The results obtained during the first step of this integration are presented and compared to those obtained with the previous vision system. These new results are encouraging and rich in lessons for the future.

Keywords: edge computing, precision agriculture, smart agriculture, automatic weeding, image processing, deep learning.

6.1 Introduction

Agriculture has to face many challenges in the 21st century. With the increasing artificialization of land and the augmentation of the global population, we have to produce more food using less surface. Another challenge in order to

DOI: 10.1201/9788743808633-6

preserve our natural resources and soil quality for agriculture, is to produce differently, with less inputs (fertilizers, phytosanitary products, herbicides...). In addition, climate change has a huge impact on production, yields, water availability and many more aspects.

To address those challenges, several solutions can be proposed, among which are smart farming, the usage of digital technologies in agriculture and precision agriculture, which can be summarised as applying to the crops the appropriate action, at the best moment, and at the right place and quantity.

In order to make those improvements in crop management, two key technologies can provide a significant help: in-field connected sensors and robotic processing of the crops.

In-field connected sensors have proven to be very useful for collecting data on the plots (vegetation index, soil composition, weather parameters...). These data are then processed and integrated in decision support systems to help the farmer manage the crops. Installing sensors in the field is not an easy task: outdoor conditions require robust material that can resist moisture, dust and shocks. Moreover, access to a power supply is not practical, so it is important to have low consumption devices, which limits the processing power available. Cloud computing could offer a solution: the sensor sends the data via internet in order to process it on a server. However, internet access is often limited in the fields and the amount of data can be large (images or videos). Another solution could be to use a long-range technology such as LoRa or SigFox. However, those technologies have a limited data rate and can't support huge amounts of data to send in the cloud.

Edge computing is a promising alternative, with the possibility to make computing on board, dramatically reducing the amount of data to be send (only the results), via LoRa for example. This makes it possible to use a connected sensor even in areas with poor network access. It also allows to reduce the power consumption involved in the communication in case of large amount of data. However, this latter advantage can be neutralized by the energy cost of the calculations carried out on board.

In the case of robotic processing of the crops, embedded sensors are necessary to provide real-time data to the system so that it can implement the operations needed to process the culture. This real time constraint favours the edge architecture, avoiding loss of time in data transfer and reception of results, especially for significant input data quantity (image or video).

In both cases, the constraints are similar: processing signals, images or videos of natural scenes require complex computations; the return on investment expected for the farmers limits the cost of the technologies used, and the lack of availability of both network and energy imposes a certain electrical and communication frugality. Therefore, the edge architectures to be deployed in such use-cases must rely on low-cost circuits, capable of implementing the most efficient algorithms – such as deep learning based neural networks – with low power consumption.

The purpose of the European project ANDANTE is to create such circuits and to test them in various real-life situations, among which smart agriculture use cases.

In this paper, we will focus on a specific smart agriculture device: a mobile vision system dedicated to the perception task of an automatic weeding tool for market gardening (BIPBIP).

The paper will be organised as follows: Section 2, "Material and methods", will describe the system. Section 3, "Reference results" will show the results obtained before the integration of ANDANTE circuits. Section 4 will show some results already obtained and will discuss the next steps.

6.2 Material and Methods

6.2.1 BIPBIP: the automatic weeding system

The automatic weeding use case within the ANDANTE project was based on the BIPBIP system developed in a previous project [1, 2]. BIPBIP is a precision weeding module designed to weed maize and bean crops in the intra-row without using any phytosanitary products. The state of the art of the weeding systems is illustrated in Figure 6.1.

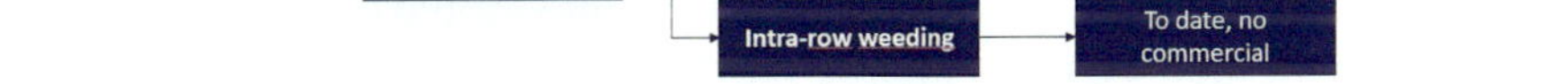

Figure 6.1 State of the art of the weeding systems.

To date, commercial intra-solution mechanical weeding solutions exists like the IC-weeder Lemkem [3], the RoboCrop InRow from Garford [4] or even the Robovator from VisionWeeding [5]. Those solutions are adapted for lettuce, cabbage, celery etc, that are crops with higher distance between two plants, as opposed to beans and maize, that have small inter-plant gap, making the intra-row weeding more challenging (geometric precision, leaf overlapping, weed and crop closer and more difficult to differentiate, etc.)

Figure 6.2 Left: BIPBIP weeding system behind a robotized tractor. Right: Inside BIPBIP, the camera and the lighting system [2].

BIPBIP is composed of a vision system that detects crops and locate crop stems and of a mechanical weeding tool (Figure 6.2 left). It targets market gardening crops such as bean, and field crops with large intra-row spacing such as maize. A similar vision-based approach is described in [6] but on lettuce and in laboratory conditions. Other approach exists like GPS-based weeding on tomato crop [7] but won't be integrated in our use case.

The system speed is 0.5 m/s. The mechanical weeding tool is composed of a metal tip that scraps the soil to remove all weeds without distinction around each plant of interest. Therefore, detecting weeds is not required for hoeing, only the crop stem positions need to be known as they are the only part of the crops to be avoided by the mechanical weeding system.

6.2.2 BIPBIP vision system

This crop detection system of the weeding module should operate in real-time and provide the stem position of crops with a great location accuracy which is required for the precision hoeing process. It is mainly based on one detector to identify the crop of interest and a second one to locate precisely its stem. These two detectors are intended to be transferred to the circuits developed in the ANDANTE project.

The initial implementation was done using a 3 megapixels RGB camera which can capture images at a rate of 15 frames per second. The camera is

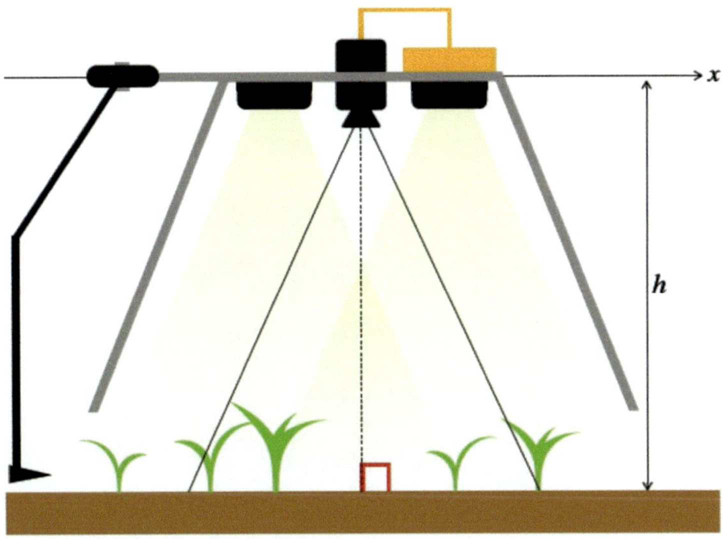

Figure 6.3 BIPBIP weeding module. The mechanical intra-row hoeing tool is represented by the rod on the left, the computing system in yellow, the two LED panels and the camera in black inside the vision chamber (in gray) which allows to isolate the vision system from changing light conditions [2].

confined in a hull avoiding natural lighting. Light conditions are controlled by 2 LED panels (Figure 6.2 right, Figure 6.3). The images are processed in real time on an NVIDIA Jetson Xavier which should be replaced by the ANDANTE board when available. The algorithms are developed in Python and deployed in C++ for faster processing speed. The software framework used for the neural network inference is written in C++ and CUDA. The detectors implemented in the weeding tool were based on a convolutional neural network YOLOv4 [8]. This model was chosen for its accuracy and speed. Indeed, the weeding operation needs to be very precise as the farmers cannot afford to lose a significant percentage of the crop during the weeding. Besides, the detection needs to be fast, as the image needs to be processed between the image acquisition and weeding operation. This allows a processing time on the embedded device within 50ms.

Regarding the training of the network, we used 4 databases (2 for maize and 2 for bean) composed of 15 fps videos saved as consecutive frames. These databases were annotated with bounding box ground-truths to provide labels for the neural network training and for the evaluation. The crop bounding

Table 6.1 Number of images and annotations for each crop.

Label	Images	Crop annotations	Stem annotations
Maize	1 034	2 095	2 133
Bean	748	2 820	2 824
Total	1 782	4 915	4 957

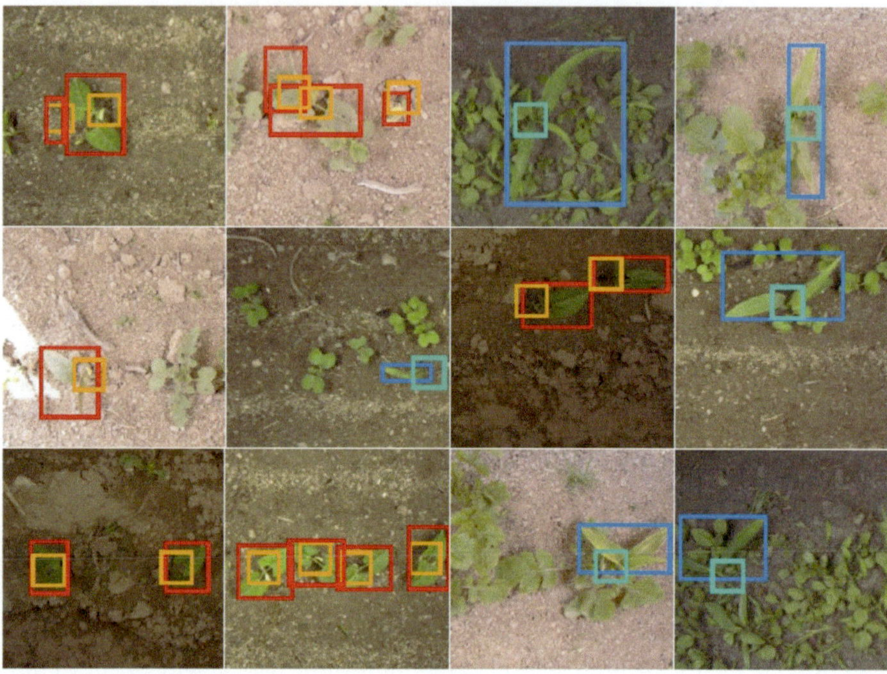

Figure 6.4 Example of annotations on the image database. Maize crops are annotated in blue and the stems in cyan, bean crops in red and the stems in orange [2].

box surround the whole crop (red and blue boxes in Figure 6.4) while the stem bounding box is centred on the stem entry point (orange and cyan boxes in Figure 6.4). Table 6.1 gives the number of images and annotations per crop.

6.2.3 ANDANTE board integration

Our objective is to replace the NVIDIA Jetson Xavier computing system by the IA accelerator board and circuit developed in ANDANTE project, and to evaluate the performances of the resulting system. Figure 6.5 illustrates the

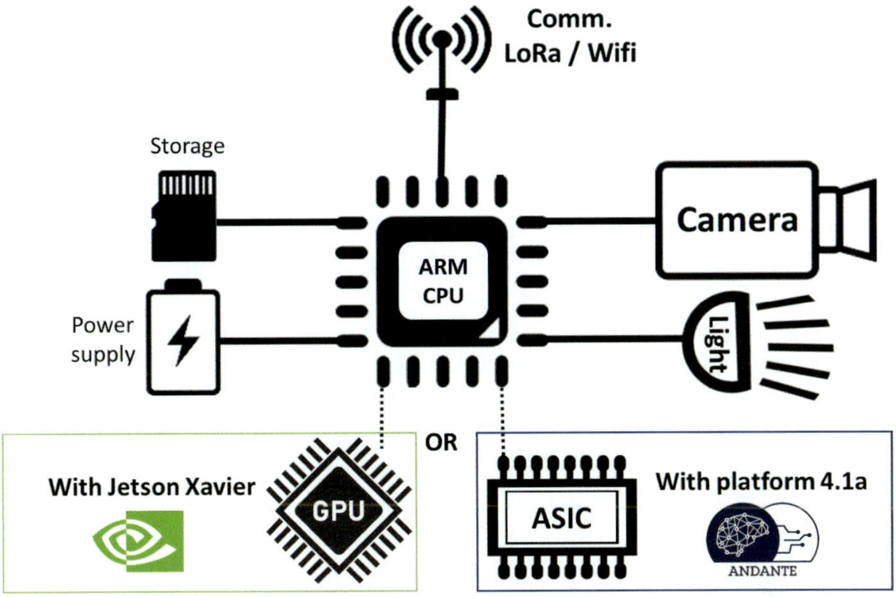

Figure 6.5 Schematic representation of the BIPBIP vision system with both hardware accelerator possible: a GPU for the NVIDIA Jetson case or an ASIC for the platform 4.1a.

future place of the ANDANTE board (*Platform 4.1a*) in the BIPBIP vision system.

The ANDANTE board consists of the NeuroCorgi [9, 10] ASIC and a Kria KV260 FPGA, running the network backbone and detection head respectively. The NeuroCorgi circuit implements a Mobilenet v1 network backbone [11]. The encoder uses hard-coded weights trained on the COCO dataset. The weights are quantized on 8-bit integers to lower the memory requirements and speed up the computation. To keep the possibility to adapt the circuit to different use cases, the FPGA is programmable and is able to run a PetaLinux distribution in order to deploy different software easily. The plant detection is performed by an SSD-Lite type head, providing similar results to the SSD detector [12] with a much lower number of parameters, by replacing the convolution layers by separable 2D convolution. The head of the SSDLite network uses 4M parameters, about half than the full SSD network's 8M parameters. This reduces the memory requirement and the computational cost for the network.

The NeuroCorgi circuit provides access to four layers of the encoder at different scales, to provide data at different levels of encoding. The output layers are taken right before the down-sampling operations (max pooling). This allows the network head to access features of various resolutions and complexity.

6.3 Reference Results

In this section, we focus on the results obtained in the initial version of the BIPBIP vision system, with the NVIDIA Jetson board in order to get reference for comparison with the future vision system with the ANDANTE board. To date, the results of the ANDANTE board are from a simulated environment, with the SSDLite running on a classical computer. We split the image database in a training set and a validation set with an 80%-20% ratio.

In terms of power consumption, the current system work around 30W. In the case of the weeding platform, power consumption isn't a critical point. Having a system consuming less power, like the ANDANTE platform, is much more beneficial regarding energy sobriety and transferring for other IoT devices such as in field sensors for which it provides a much higher autonomy.

Table 6.2 Detection performance (%) and inference speed (fps) for Yolo v4 on the NVIDIA Jetson Xavier including video acquisition and post-processing for each crop.

Network	AP	AP_{50}	AP_{75}	mIOU	FPS
Yolo V4	53.87	89.71	54.59	80.96	13
SSDLite	51.6	84.6	52	80.5	N/A

Table 6.2 shows the performance using AP0.5:0.95 (AP), the AP50, AP75, AR100, the mean Intersection over Union (mIoU) [13] and the inference speed in frames per second (FPS). The YoloV4 results previously obtained gives us a reference for this use case. We can observe similar results with the SSDLite, which is satisfactory but on condition of an acceptable inference speed. However, as the SSDLite is running in a simulated environment, it isn't relevant to measure the number of FPS for this network. When available, the processing speed should allow at least 10 FPS.

Detailed results can be found in [1, 2].

6.4 Work in Progress and Future Work

6.4.1 Work in progress

Since the ANDANTE *Platform 4.1a* is not yet available, our network architecture described in section 1.2 has been implemented and tested using the available development tools. The Mobilenet-based SSD detector was implemented using the Pytorch library, with separate classes for the backbone and the detection head. A simulator for the NeuroCorgi circuit was implemented on the N2D2 platform [14], which is a deep learning framework for creating artificial neural networks intended to work on constrained environments. The SSD network head was translated for the Kria KV260 FPGA using the VitisAI library.

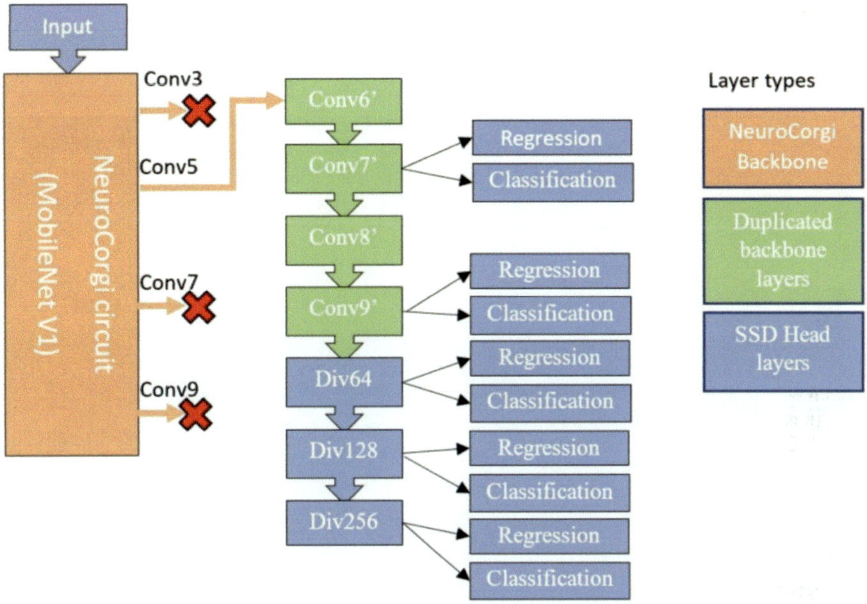

Figure 6.6 The adapted network architecture used for this application. The figure presents how the duplicated Mobilenet layers and the SSD head are connected to the NeuroCorgi backbone.

Some modifications to the network structure were necessary: as the training database for the encoder contains few examples of plants, the initial detection results were inadequate. Duplicating some of the encoder layers on the FPGA and making them trainable improved considerably the detection accuracy. The resulting network architecture is presented in Figure 6.6.

Table 6.3 shows the first results from the proposed architecture (these results are expressed in terms of loss function but the precision performances will be available soon). These results are promising, even if the SSD architecture is less precise that the reference Yolo V4 network. They also show that it is necessary to use at least a partially retrained backbone. However, the improvement after retraining the first layers is marginal.

Table 6.3 Detection performance (loss function) using the new architecture.

Network training	Loss on SSD	Loss on SSD Lite
Head only	3.8	4.6
Partially retrained backbone	1.8	1.9
Retrained backbone	1.5	1.7

Figure 6.7 presents examples of detection obtained by the reference system and by the proposed network.

Figure 6.7 Results from the Yolo V4 network (left) and the proposed SSD network (right) on maize. Blue rectangles show the plants. Green rectangles show the stem locations.

6.4.2 Future work

The two parts of the network are currently being transferred on the *Platform 4.1a*. The performances, in terms of accuracy, processing time and power consumption will then be measured and compared to the reference (NVIDIA Jetson Xavier board). If the accuracy and computing time are adequate, the implementation inside the BIPBIP weeding system will then be possible, allowing field testing.

6.5 Conclusion

In this paper we presented a vision system for automatic weeding (BIPBIP platform), and described the objectives and the progress of a project to evolve this vision system, through the integration of an Artificial Intelligence oriented computation board with low cost and low power consumption (ANDANTE project).

The existing vision system (BIPBIP) should allow easy hardware integration by replacing the NVIDIA Jetson Xavier with the new circuit. However, an adaptation of the Convolutional Neural Network model appeared to be necessary. Encouraging simulations have shown the overall feasibility of the transfer, and have been very informative, particularly about the need to adapt the initial architecture of the circuit to achieve the expected precision performance expected for weed control applications.

Furthermore, the availability of the new ANDANTE circuit makes it possible to address other "smart agriculture" use case such as a fixed vineyard monitoring vision sensor. The integration of the new ANDANTE board, even in its current architecture, should make it possible to improve the very simple vision processing algorithms carried out on board the existing prototype, while keeping a low power consumption inherent to this type of device, thus allowing to extend its uses.

Acknowledgements

The ANDANTE project has received funding from the ECSEL Joint Undertaking (JU) under grant agreement No 876925. The JU receives support from the European Union's Horizon 2020 research and innovation programme and Belgium, France, Germany, The Netherlands, Portugal, Spain, Switzerland. www.andante-ai.eu.

The BIPBIP project has been funded by the French Research Agency (ANR) (grant ANR-17-ROSE-0001 - BIPBIP) and has been supported by the organizers of the ROSE Challenge and all the partners of the BIPBIP project.

Index

About the Editors

Dr. Ovidiu Vermesan holds a PhD degree in microelectronics and a Master of International Business (MIB) degree. He is Chief Scientist at SINTEF Digital, Oslo, Norway. His research interests are intelligent systems integration, mixed-signal embedded electronics, analogue neural networks, edge artificial intelligence and cognitive communication systems. Dr. Vermesan received SINTEF's 2003 award for research excellence for his work on implementing a biometric sensor system. He is currently working on projects addressing nanoelectronics, integrated sensor/actuator systems, communication, cyber-physical systems (CPSs) and the Industrial Internet of Things (IIoT), with applications in green mobility, energy, autonomous systems, and smart cities. He has authored or co-authored over 100 technical articles and conference papers. He is actively involved in the activities of the European partnership for Key Digital Technologies (KDT) Joint Undertaking (JU), now the Chips JU. He has coordinated and managed various national, EU and other international projects related to smart sensor systems, integrated electronics, electromobility and intelligent autonomous systems such as E3Car, POLLUX, CASTOR, IoE, MIRANDELA, IoF2020, AUTOPILOT, AutoDrive, ArchitectECA2030, AI4DI, AI4CSM. Dr. Vermesan actively participates in national, Horizon Europe and other international initiatives by coordinating and managing various projects. He is a member of the Alliance for AI, IoT and Edge Continuum Innovation (AIOTI) board. He is currently the coordinator of the Edge AI Technologies for Optimised Performance Embedded Processing (EdgeAI) project.

Marcello Coppola is technical Director at STMicroelectronics. He has more than 25 years of industry experience with an extended network within the research community and major funding agencies with the primary focus on the development of break-through technologies. He is a technology innovator, with the ability to accurately predict technology trends. He is involved in many European research projects targeting Industrial IoT and IoT, cyber physical systems, Smart Agriculture, AI, Low power, Security, 5G, and design technologies for Multicore and Many-core System-on-Chip, with particular emphasis to architecture and network-on-chip. He has published more than 50 scientific publications, holds over 26 issued patents. He authored chapters in 12 edited print books, and he is one of the main authors of "Design of Cost-Efficient Interconnect Processing Units: Spidergon STNoC" book. Until 2018, he was part of IEEE Computing Now Journal Technical editorial board. He contributed to the security chapter of the Strategic Research Agenda (SRA) to set the scene on R&I on Embedded Intelligent Systems in Europe. He is serving under different roles numerous top international conferences and workshops. Graduated in Computer Science from the University of Pisa, Italy in 1992.

Dr. Fabian Chersi has a BSC and a master's in electronic physics, and a PhD in Artificial Intelligence and Robotics. From 2001 to 2003, he worked as a researcher at the Technical University of Munich, Germany, at the department of Robotics and Embedded Systems. From 2003 to 2007, he worked at the University of Parma and of Minho on the neurophysiological experiments with monkeys, and the development of biologically realistic models of the mirror neuron system and on the development of biologically inspired robotic systems. From 2007 to 2009, he did a Postdoc at the Institute for Neuroinformatics in Zurich and at the University College of in London on the development of attractor networks for context dependent reasoning and mental state transitions. From to 2009 he was working at the National Council for Research in Rome, on the development of biologically inspired models of the cortico-basal ganglia system for goal-directed and habitual action execution and of the hypothalamus-striatum circuit for spatial navigation. He then moved to Paris where he worked on the development of neuromorphic algorithms and ASICs for deep neural networks. He currently works at the Commission for Atomic and Alternative Energies Commission (CEA) in Paris as a senior AI architect on DNN optimization and low power AI chips for the edge.

For Product Safety Concerns and Information please contact our
EU representative GPSR@taylorandfrancis.com Taylor & Francis
Verlag GmbH, Kaufingerstraße 24, 80331 München, Germany